# Unisex Love Poems

ANGELA SZCZEPANIAK

# Unisex Love Poems

LIVRES
DC
BOOKS

Cover art by Jeff Szuc.
Author photograph by Julian Baxter.
Book designed and typeset by Primeau & Barey, Montreal.
Edited by Jason Camlot for the Punchy Writers Series.

Copyright © Angela Szczepaniak, 2008.
Legal Deposit, *Bibliothèque et Archives nationales du Québec*
and the National Library of Canada, 4th trimester, 2008.

Library and Archives Canada Cataloguing in Publication
Szczepaniak, Angela, 1975-
Unisex love poems/Angela Szczepaniak.
ISBN 978-1-897190-40-1 (bound).
ISBN 978-1-897190-39-5 (pbk.)
I. Title.
PS8637.Z39U55 2008 C811'.6 C2008-906476-3

For our publishing activities, DC Books gratefully acknowledges the financial
support of the Canada Council for the Arts, of SODEC, and of the Government
of Canada through the Book Publishing Industry Development Program (BPIDP).

**Canada Council
for the Arts**   **Conseil des Arts
du Canada**   *Société
de développement
des entreprises
culturelles*
Québec

Printed and bound in Canada by Marquis Imprimeur. Interior pages printed
on 100 per cent recycled and FSC certified Silva Enviro white paper.
Distributed by LitDistCo.

DC Books
PO Box 666, Station Saint-Laurent
Montreal, Quebec H4L 4V9
www.dcbooks.ca

*for 201*

## *on snatching your chance*

Arrange it so the girl is sitting at the arm of the divan–she will feel at ease with the security of plumply stuffed silk upholstery and so positioned will not be as supple of movement to allow wriggling away from your approach. Tread softly, mind, in spite of any possible hints of tumescence twinging beneath your skin; take for granted that your mark will be of limited osculation experience. It is best to begin by working into it with some gallant pretense such as adjusting the lampshade or some small cushion for her comfort. The fairer sex appreciates such gestures of modern chivalry. Take the melting gratitude of her coy cherrylips framing pearly teeth as your opportunity to glide in for that all important seal of love, the tender brush of your lip to hers.

***4f corridor    slug    straightens shirt    smoothes hair with
a palm    refers to notecards    levels three sharp knocks***

SLUG: OK 4f. Let's get a couple of things out of the way up
front. You're butterfingers, right? Your mailbox says butter-
fingers…. That's correct? Well, 4f. butterfingers. I've been
working my way through the building and it seems that
most people have concerns that fall into three groups when
I knock on a door.

First: I'm not selling anything. I don't want any money
from you or other commitments of that nature and I'm not
going to demonstrate a revolutionary product of any kind.
No vacuum cleaner blender sandwich maker milkshake
machine portable sewing unit. No investment portfolios
plans for advance burial plot selection pyramid schemes.
Nothing like any of that.

Two: This has nothing to do with lunacy. I am a little
under the weather, which I'll explain shortly. But not
mad. And probably not contagious. It's important to
your mental comfort for the next few minutes that you
remember that.

And finally: I'm not from a religious organization cult or
small sect of worshippers who thrive on conversion and/or
donation. I have no interest in evangelizing the various
paradises salvations or apocalypses available to us through
any of the religious doctrines we are invited to hedge our
bets with. Though my dermatological issues most likely
have apocalyptic resonances in their own way.

Pardon me taking my shirt off for a moment.

Look at this–you can follow the lines, the gentle curve with a finepoint fingertip. And the itching. Beautifully repugnant. Stinging satisfaction at every scrape of the nail. I'm completely broken out in this... rash... this rash of *h*'s. Woke up with it like a bolt. Felt like a bite... mosquito, though they're out of season, I guess. Spider maybe. Mites. But turns out... an *h*-rash. Raising the skin in weeping puffs. Delicious prickling itches, all haphazard across the belly. Grotesquely alphabetic viral wallpaper. At least it's had the decency to relegate itself to the torso. It's all you can really hope for in a day. That bit of decency you can pick up here and there, even as your own body betrays you.

The cause must be somewhere in our building–possibly embedded within the construction itself. Sick building syndrome. Contagious architecture. Some microscopic... creature... in the scaffolding is hosting off us.

So what I'll need from you is this: A list of any unusual symptoms you may have been experiencing recently–anything at all... no twitch is too small to report. Any mysterious itches bumps patches fevers aches or other stiff-nesses swelling bruises coughs sneezes goosebumps dreams thoughts speeches or conversations (alone or with others). And anything else you can't account for.

Compile your unaccountables and discrepancies and slip it through my letterbox. 5d.

And I'd like to have a look around your apartment too if you don't mind–to see any suspicious (but likely inconspicuous) cracks or flourishing collections of moulds... edificial contaminants of that sort.

I mean, it's for all our benefit. But you'd be surprised at how many of our neighbours do mind.

Well, we'll see who's there to pick up the pieces of their shattered and prickled weeping epidermises when they fall into their own oozing alphabetic ruin.

## *"open house"*
## *featuring butterfingers, our plucky tightrope walking heroine*

mind your head

tightrope lower than first appears

sleight of eye     from the overside you can balance on
the flat of a well chalked fingertip   one knee crooked a crisp forty five
toe pointed for grace and logistics
encounter the world inverted     assists digestion
and  organization of coping mechanisms
a gingerpear confection

if you look to the left     you'll see

triptych of a typist's hands     hovering
alphabetic action  imminent
empty symbol     if you're the sort who's looking
feel free to inspect the cracks     beneath glint frames     however

to the right
several collectibles of the spaceage
intricate assemblage     of plastic and taste

closet     regular     beyond comment   one can plainly see
but   you  require  indulgence  here
three sections     of costuming and frippery
for the street  and  other performances

marmalades    ostrich feathers    baroque pearls
suspended upon lilac scent    separated pin neat
by hand painted microcanvasses
stunning feats of calligraphy   which graphologists   would invest with
devotion to unnecessaries   (conspicuous flair at $q$'s tail)


defunct fireplace    boot closet    bathroom


kitchen    the potbelly stainless is the best   if pressed to choose  but
they all lack    teapots for one
and other domestic    housewarming implements


pantry    a marvel of   shoebox chronology
stacked trim   efficient
discrete units    divided by acquaintance
ticket stubs    blotted napkins    clipped hair    matchbooks
miscellaneous relationship dna
catalogued    stamped    salted away   for future reference

## *"diagnostic"*
## *featuring a weft rapport*

SLUG:    So

Have you always had that... stutter?


BUTTERFINGERS:    well you   know how it is when   you
talk a lot but  aren't   skilled at   conversation
words tumbling together   pellets funneling
through papier-mâché  punctured


SLUG:    Right. But is it... new?


BUTTERFINGERS:    relatively   but not   unwelcome
all the detached speech   remnants of colloquy  drifting
through the air   floating   to the heart   of the drum
wawawa girl troubles   wawawawa  syrupy vocals over wa
scraps of chatter  slide into the ear  fishes finicking  in buttercup lobes
silly whisper juice   blueing lips  at the edges


SLUG:    This is definitely something we should investigate. It's like a
stutter but not. It's more of a... verbal *rash*. A symptom!


BUTTERFINGERS:    but   prettier than most  all gawk and awe
poised
featherlight and twitched

flashfried nouns     trip  crisp     flutter     clean and sharp
picric versatility of the word     lends
shape and articulation


SLUG:     Spectacular.
I knew we were on the cusp of other... afflictions. I knew it.
I'm right on top of it. I've got a plan at least. It's still a bit ad hoc,
but, well, we'll get a tape recorder–don't look alarmed, it's just
to cross-reference with my other data.

This is a beautiful discovery. Thrilling. We'll take samples
and swabs. Grow your rogue syllable segments in Petri dishes.
Examine cultures under microscopes.

I need to enter you into the database while it's fresh. I'll be
in touch.

*floors run by on elevator dial    coquettish*

BUTTERFINGERS:

       hey chicken cat   munch this
    two ferrets stumble out of a bar   dewyeyed
softpack black bart   snapping  under teeth   yellowwash
  each thinking   he's cleverer than the other   get it?

***hands clasped behind   foot tapping   unfortunate fidgetry***

SLUG:   Watch your step. Wow. That clumsiness must be a real...
professional hazard... your line of work, and everything.

I'm glad I ran into you. I've been wanting to check on your....
I mean, on how you are....
Symptomwise.
But I wasn't sure....
I mean, I've been so... busy.

I've been getting a lot done, though. You'd be surprised
how intricate this place is. Really. It's just nook after crack,
all swimming with disease. So the investigation's going
well on that score.

Nice buttons.
On your coat, I mean.
You know...
... the real problem is that no one has proper respect for buttons
anymore. There was a time.... I'm sure of it.... I don't remember it,
of course... but I'm sure there was a time when a good button
gave people pause. Real pause.
Gasps even. Now that's the kind of thing I'm talking about.
A button that makes you gasp with its precision and cool
anglelessness. The surfaceness of it.

*field notes     apartment 5d*
*recorded by slug*
*evidence collected to determine the cause of the h-rash*

SUBJECT 42: brown moth

PHYSICAL CHARACTERISTICS
    weightless    flimsy
    delicate     in spite of bilgebrown hue
    papery wings   vein-crimped
    twittering landing   but
    stately glide     (contributes to air of smugness)


BEHAVIOUR
    constant (nocturnal) movement   quick   sharp
    settles on ceiling one hundred eight to two hundred forty three
        times daily
        for purposes… still under scrutiny
    civilized dining habits
        (dainty of mouthparts)
    favours polyvinyl chloride over softened fabrics
        moments of still and watching       unknown targets
    uncooperative during urine sample collection
        (renders observer suspicious)


RESPONSE TO STIMULI
    drawn to light
        (artificial and flame   indiscriminate)
    flutters at loud noises   extreme heat   the sudden movement
        of shadows
    engages evasive maneuvering   at swatting   swiping
        squashing

cringes at contact with water droplets
    and mentions of its mother
avoids contact with marsupial portraits on west wall
    (likely due to revulsion)
sheds single tear at thought of own mortality

CONTACT WITH $h$'s (IN RASH FORM)
    no perceptible recognition or change in behaviour

PRELIMINARY CONCLUSIONS
    chilled by apathy    flat indifference
    not likely transmitter of dermatological contagion

### 5d    *towel wrapped   considering*

SLUG:    Ridiculous. How am I supposed to get this
hydrocortisone on my spine? This is why, well one
reason…. A major factor to consider, you know…
to pairing. So when you get plastered in *h*'s there's
someone there to balm it down.
Pathetic. Really pathetic. That it comes down to
a matter of salves.

## warm absent day

BUTTERFINGERS:


feet blister most earnestly    at the heel        white    fluidfilled
prick with gleaming pin    to allow for slow    leaking    nail slipped in
   widen with wriggling    pinch wet skin    thumb and index    pull
   considered  thin strips    tear off the sole        pull
      harder    faster
        layered  leaves of flesh    vary   in degrees of thickness
      curl fingernails under spongy seam
                              split         lift
unwrap tissue  and  sinew   a sticky sheet    follow veins with fingertip
  map out the ends of nerves  pale ligaments  crystal blue  rosebud red
        step down and back        press firmly    warm concrete
            moist new prints
                          dry with care in tepid sun

but     my peels are multidimensional
with      their whites and violets     yellownumberfives
raw colours      faded      as they do


enter     the prickling sigh for      ladies' magazines that really
work     that really open into something      some
glossy manageability     to colourfast the days' seams      crisp
the edges      deferring inevitable frays and bleeds

### *on dodging the inevitable rogue hand*

Nice girls need not feel the pressure to pet. Petting as the price of
popularity is far too dear for the girl of suitable taste and refinement.
*Ladies* need not in the least be stamped prudes on grounds of refusing
to pet, or for frowning on all forms of petting. Common sense
and a little cleverness is all the decent girl need rely upon to duck
unwelcome or presumptuous petting. Simultaneous petting and
drinking, or a like calibre of cheap conduct, are, needless to remind
you dear girls, apt to lead to further promises of promiscuity.

was in love with a     cellist once     had     beautiful hands
                   pickpocket slender          supple
fingers floated over flesh  with     spider delicacy     precision

          everything you'd expect; catgut seduction


          acid on the tongue     words tart     undissolved
laced up tight  to the throat  razorcut     edges barely perceptible
                   lying flat at the seam

the many fascinations of domesticity   take over

from time to time

causing fleeting attempts at   homecookery   revolutionary methods
of dusting
and oven cleaning    propelled by unwarranted nidification verve
days waft away       under
captivating bouquets of    bleaches and simulated lemons
head stuffed with       cottonwool daydreams

culinary sculpture ensues

radish rosettes   carving perfection fulfilled   by under water blooming
daisied carrots  smug with westinghouse chill  garnish pride blossoms
moussed salmon pinwheels   spin promises   of eloquence
and sophistication
for educated palates   encouragement for
experienced tongues

tell it to the tooth

through window gauze       delightful haze  of outdoors       settles
inspired activities       betty emily donna june       striving for
extraordinary innovation in     the field of slow cooking
demanding astonishing commitment to     friendship fairy cakes
lauded to the nets       unprecedented combinations of
baked hams   radiant   honeydew drops   ringed pineapples
planned over and     over afternoon biscuits

laudanum scripts

materialize     the darling of cocktail parties
purveyor of crystalbright dinner chatter     exquisite graceries
falling  petalhard into      intoxicating porcelains  decaled  whitened
brittled     with rose ribbons     and boiled bone

## Stuffed *Cœur*

**butter
(browned)**

**parsley
(lavishly torn)**

**mace blades
(pounded)**

**honey
(drizzled)**

**bay leaves
(ironed)**

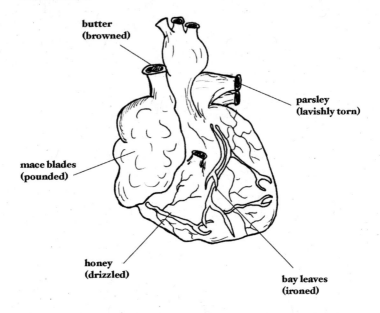

## *mode*

Bathe hearts[1] in salty tepid water until
excess blood drains[2]
Trim visible fat and functions
Bind sweetened onion, breadcrumbs,
and spices with egg
Wad stuffing into ventricles, atria, and
other available cavities
Secure chambers with toothpicks
or a bejewelled hatpin[3]
Lay in warm stewing fluid to ovenroast

---

1 A pair of large vigorous hearts will answer nicely for an intimate syncytium
  feast for two.
2 The heart bath will turn a lovely crimson hue, which can be used to set
  atmosphere and tone in your diningroom; simply pour into a decorative
  crystal carafe or vase for fragrant lilac blossoms.
3 Stuffed hearts needn't be securely fastened, though generally, the more care
  one puts into closure, the greater her affection for her dining companion.
  The industrious and devoted honeydrop will use strands of her own hair
  to sew cavities.

## on chirping the canary

The necessity of being a good conversationalist hardly
needs to be elaborated upon here. However, take care to
note that what appears to be effortless chatter comes from
the strong root of preparation and practice in the art of
feminine conversation. A sharp dialogist always appears
witty, charming, and engaging. But one need not find these
admirable qualities daunting. What one lacks by nature's
hand can be garnered from the more refined manuals.
The truly intelligent girl will prepare no less than *five* literary
quotations to contribute to her suitor's musings. It is best
to learn two all-purpose Shakespeares, a solid Wordsworth,
a Liz Browning for grace, and a Keats or Shelley to round
things out. It is also on form (and will no doubt impress) to
discover his favourite author and tuck a quotation or two
culled from this source in the bib of your bodice. Sadly, it
is not enough to have this body of references on hand. One
must, unless she wishes to appear silly or dull witted, know
when to *deploy* these famous words (refer to appendix 3A
at the back of this volume for a listing of quotations and
appropriate contexts in which to insert them). Keeping
abreast of major current events will allow the clever girl to
commit an agreeable nod in accordance with her beau's
opinions, or sparingly, a more definitive "why, certainly."
Care must be taken not to overannotate. One must keep
in mind that the best conversationalist is, above all, a good
listener and a judicious speaker. Think how surprised you
would be, dear girls, to hear your pretty canary answer
you back!

## *scraps: a dinnerdate*

SLUG:    Can I have your skin?
I mean, if you're not going to eat it.
It's just.... It's so
Tantalizing. Sitting there at the edge of your plate....
Glistening by the tealight.... Crisp burnt edges. Curled
back black... brown... pink. The curve of pearlescent
underside delicately bubbled... waiting.

## Rasher Rolls off the Tongue

### *mode*

Pound the body of a meaty tongue
(roughly six muscular pounds)
Scrape tasting surface to slough visible tastebuds
Core deeply rooted papillae and salivary glands
with the tip of a finepoint fingerblade
Extract stubborn buds and gristle webbing
with tweezers
Score dorsal side of flesh, allowing excess blood
and fluid drainage
Lay bacon rashers lengthwise under tongue
Pinwheel into a hefty roll
Drape with fatnet to flavour roast
Garnish with crispfried tastebud extractions

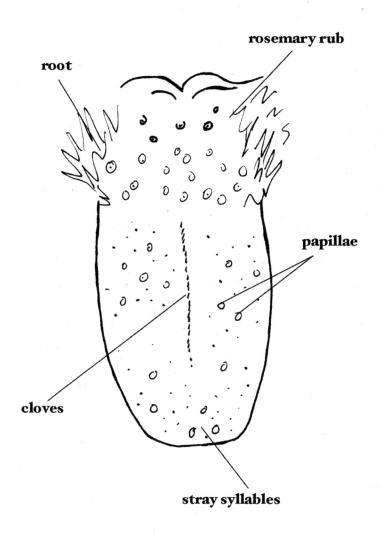

root

rosemary rub

papillae

cloves

stray syllables

## "I wonder what fool it was that invented kissing"
*Jonathan Swift*

Fool indeed! What Mr Swift must have been thinking when he dribbled this aphorism, one can scarcely guess. Though navigating the female mind may prove trying at times, remember the high voltage jolt, searing bliss skull to toe, when one finds that his gentlemanly efforts have taken route. Imagine courtship without the kiss. How dull a dinnerdate would be minus the promise of a goodnight peck to seal the evening sweet. What carrot would dangle to lead the fine gentleman through the slog of attending the theatre, the panto, the symphony; of listening to natterings about flowers and frippery and seashells; of attending family singalongs by the fire, if the promise of osculation were brutally ripped from his expectations? How would one measure success without the appropriate progress from the peck to the smooch to the snog and on? Why, without the hope of the lip we'd all end up in card dens and saloons, refusing gifts of handpicked peach preserves and amateur watercolours from prospective paramours, in favour of spirits and cigars with the lads, or worse, darkening the local tom shops to secure reliable buccal favours. The fool, clearly, is the one bent to miss the kiss, for what other reward is there to profit from our exertion and ingenuity?

*field notes     apartment 5d*
*recorded by slug*
*evidence collected to determine the cause of the h-rash*

SUBJECT 47: window pigeon (urban)


PHYSICAL CHARACTERISTICS
   predominant colouring     fiery ginger     white flecks
      (tail feather concentration)
   oil streaked     vermin infested (microscopic louse variety)
   chest puffed (playful swagger     overcompensating)
   right leg   crimson    fully intact (apparently normal)
      left    clawfoot clubbed ominous     gumshoed
   eyes    glassyblack     excessively pupilled
      (arousing discomfort     suspicion)


BEHAVIOUR
   advances coquettish strut across windowsill
      (3-6 hours daily     cumulative)
   interpretative tic     cocks head right     thought settling
   prone to frequent acts of fecal vandalism
      (favours south railing     for its ornateness   possibly)
   gazes with longing    into livingroom window
   balances gracefully     on right foot    (sunrise/sunset)


RESPONSE TO STIMULI
   coos at sight of:     fluffed kittens
                         boiled humbugs
                         own reflection (off-putting lack of humility)
   exhibits striking preoccupation with foodstuffs:
      spits sunflower husks into orderly piles
         (with other indigestibles)

27

pecks at currant teacakes   and mint frosted petits fours
refuses    birdseed   breadcrumbs   and like offerings
squints at:   bright lights   blinking neon
eyedroppers of water   red fruit juices   liquid gelatin   et cetera
discharged on or near face and neck
perceptible wink at     direct eye contact
(unsettling forthright sexuality)
provides enchanting harmony and countermelody to
violin concertos
(demonstrates distinct preference for and affinity with Ravel)

CONTACT WITH $h$'S (IN RASH FORM)
maintains discreet distance
after repeated insistent contact    offers sympathetic wingbeat

PRELIMINARY CONCLUSIONS
marked    potentially obsessive    interest in observer
unable to establish direct correlation between subject and
$h$-contagion

# Larded Thymus Puffs

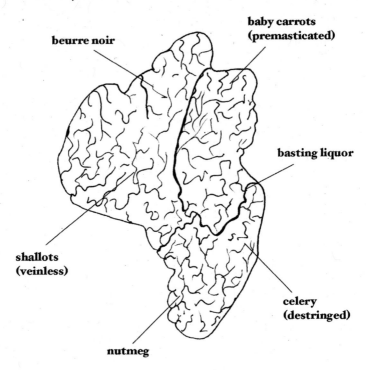

beurre noir

baby carrots
(premasticated)

basting liquor

shallots
(veinless)

celery
(destringed)

nutmeg

## mode

Chunk glands[1] into tidy morsels
Lard thickly and evenly
(fatty bacon infuses delightfully)
Lay larded thymus tidbits upon
a bed of herbed vegetables
After a sharp oven, the surface
will be brightly browned, ripe for puffing
Garnish *bonne bouches* with willowy elegance[2]

---

1 Be sure to choose the freshest available thymus parts. Those harvested from young throats yield sweeter, juicier, plumper glands that will be sure to please the tender tongues of even your most discriminating dinner guest.

2 Gland Puffs (whether larded or encrusted) make an ideal hors d'oeuvre at any of the socials you may have the delightment of hostessing... dinner parties; business cocktail affairs; showers and teas of all varieties. Dress thymus pairs with coloured sprinkles and you'll be every child's favourite birthday party gourmet!

## on exceeding flesh and bone limitations

Few of us are born into absolute physical suitability. It doesn't take much for us to see Miss Neighbour's slender ankles swanning toward her hem or Cousin Ethel's delicate hands clasped neatly in her lap, to be reminded of our own shortcomings. Though nature may be cruel in her distribution of pleasing attributes, it is a matter of etiquette and good breeding that we take measures to manage her missteps everywhere possible, regardless of our flesh and bone limitations. These days, if a girl wants to maintain her standing in polite circles she will begin by taking a good stern look at her person in the mirror. If she is truly honest with herself, it should take little effort to ascertain and catalogue each of her flaws, and set to work straight away at mending them. Often it is simply a matter of calling on the wisdom of *deportment.* For instance, in the case of pedal enormity, one need only select the appropriate shoe to complement the monstrous extremity rather than follow the latest trend at the cost of bodily decorum. How obvious this seems! Surely no one would be so foolish as to commit such a blatant corporal atrocity! If only this were true. Many a decent girl would shrink at how often one can look at Miss Hostess' clods stuffed into the most fashionable dainty slippers fancying herself the belle of her ball. Not to mention how many a fine dinner party has been pummelled to ruin by the twittering fool of a girl bent on tromping about with her great hooves spilling out of an elegant Mary Jane. Scandalous. Rest assured, there is no place for the slovenly-footed with any topcrust coterie.

entertained a snakeoil barker        once
        sold        toothpowder  and  laundry bluing
    decadent vitamin syrups  producing seven essential effects
        on imperfect bodies        purple potions    for assistance
with stain removal    balsams for ailing domesticity      at cost

eloquence dispensed in town squares

                                specializing in
        product potential      raw possibility      by the case


        rosyhued lacquer over yellowing nailbeds
        barrelchest straining complicated vest fobs
        lost wallets at dinner    trousers a hair too short

all remedied


                            caress of rolling baritone
    sumptuously hoarse      anecdotes carefully unspooled
        gravel lush    sediment sweetened tympanic
            pleasing candycoated eardrums

saw a chiropractor     by referral
meat cleaver hands     uncouth and lush     clapped dauntless
burly reassurance comforted     uncoiled the spine
corkscrewed alignment     quicksnapped vertical
swordsharp articulation of the vertebrae
head restitched in place     shivered muscular adventure


a solid contender     admitting


breezeblock lizard medicine     crisped
batwings and saltines     the spleens of several small mammals
desiccated     peeled     powdered reliable
a tingle on the tongue     triggers therapeutic delirium

*field notes     apartment 5d*
*recorded by slug*
*evidence collected to determine the cause of the h-rash*

SUBJECT 293: shower mould

PHYSICAL CHARACTERISTICS
glossy black     flourished     delicate resilience
velvet textured spiral clouds
    the figure of broccoli florets in eternal mourning
spored dandies     advancing upon damp corners     tile cracks
    well groomed microbial disaster     lurking


BEHAVIOUR
sprouts breakneck fungal civilizations
    pervasive     suffocating highrise permeation
    revealing vicious strategies of powder room domination


RESPONSE TO STIMULI
shrivels at hi-fi imbalance
    (visible annoyance with dense bass)
hisses commingling with spider plant and other greenery
    (disparages most foliage     indiscriminately     as "fern bar
    princesses")
attempted strangulation of smaller mammals
    scaled leaves curling soft necks     with hunger and intention
withstands all manner of bleaches     ammonias
    and other amped cleaning fluids
flaunts blatant disregard for scraping     sponging     descaling tactics
unresponsive to raised voice negotiations

CONTACT WITH *h*'s (IN RASH FORM)
>recoils immediately from infected areas
>>embellished disgust arouses suspicion

PRELIMINARY CONCLUSIONS
>in two to three years observer's mouldsmothered body will likely
>be discovered
>bearded with posthumous regrowth
>still papered in a moss of *h*'s

### *"the briefing"*
### *featuring spitz & spatz, the collapsible, diminutive legal duet*

SPITZ:   Just get his eye open.

SPATZ:   I'm trying…. Every time I get the lid flipped up it snaps–ow!

SPITZ:   Watch your fingers!

SPATZ:   I dunno, spitz. I think we're gonna need a prop. You got a hairpin?

SPITZ:   A hairpin! What do you take me for?

SPATZ:   Just hopeful I guess.

SPITZ:

SPATZ:   Well–do you have anything?
Go on… give your pockets a good rifle. Maybe you've stuffed a twig or something in your cummerbund.

SPITZ:   Ugh… hang on then.

Aha! Here you are, good sir.

SPATZ:   What's this? A cigarillo stump?
Oh spitz, you haven't fallen off the wagon again?

SPITZ:   I like their sweet nutty flavour. The slow curl of smoke winding through–

SPATZ:   But your poor lungs. Just fluttering away in
    your chest. Twittering like papery white moth wings–

SPITZ:   In the back.
    Hold the lid for me?

SPATZ:   What?

SPITZ:   I think they're in the back.

SPATZ:   What–lungs? Since when?

SPITZ:   Since.... I don't know. But everything can't
    be bunched into the front.
    Look, are you going to help me wedge it in or not?
    Get a good tuft of the lash.

SPATZ:   Don't suppose you've got a toothpick in your
    vest pocket?

SPITZ:   Stop being trite. Just hold the ball still so I can stick
    this stump in. We've got to get him up and moving.
    We're weeks behind as it is.
    She's already got the house sewn up.

SPATZ:   Has she?

SPITZ:   Well she must if he's living in a place like... this.

SPATZ:   Oh goodness me. I think some ash has fallen in. See it? It's just there on the white bit. Hand me your handkerchief.

SLUG:   Ugh.

SPITZ:   Watch that hand there, sprout.

SLUG:   Ugh.
*[Sniff.]*

SPATZ:   I don't think he's fully with us yet–still in the random flailing stages, my darling.

SPITZ:   I've told you about that "darling" splash. I mean it.

SPATZ:   Yes, yes. Right you are. A momentary slip of the boundary. Consider the walls firmly raised again. Not a brick out of place.

As you were.

SPITZ:   I'm sick of this primrose. I'm just gonna slap him.

SPATZ:   spitz!

SPITZ:   Just enough to rouse. Relax.

SLUG:   Ow!

SPITZ:   It's about time.

SPATZ:   Hello there, good sir.

SLUG:   What are you?

SPITZ:   Who.

SLUG:   What?

SPITZ:   No, not *what.... Who.*

SPATZ:   spatz here. At your service. And may I present
my companion, spitz.

SPITZ:   Professional associate.

SPATZ:   Go on spitz... shake hands.

SPITZ:   Show us to your files.

SLUG:   My rash–you're causing my rash. I can feel it
creeping into my eye. It feels like nails scratching... what–
A cigarette butt?

SPITZ:   Cigarillo.

SLUG:   You're ashing out in my eyes while I sleep? Is that
how you keep the rash going on and on, digging into every
edge of nerve, fraying everything just below the skin?

SPATZ:   Don't be silly. We're here to help you.

SLUG:    With my *h*'s?

SPITZ:   With your case.

SLUG:    Case? My case of *h*'s?

SPITZ:   Your *legal* case. You're in divorce proceedings, aren't you?

SLUG:    That was ages ago. It's all done now.

SPATZ:   'Fraid not. We've reopened it.

SLUG:    You can do that? What for?

SPITZ:   Unfinished business.

SLUG:    Felt pretty done to me.
         God, this thing prickles like hell.

SPITZ:   Look around you.... You really wanna finish your business... here? Like... this?

SLUG:

SPITZ:   Don't be a violet. Pick yourself up and burn that miserable monkey cup of yours in court next time.

SLUG:  Monkey cup?

SPITZ:  It's a flower, primrose.

SPATZ:  Quite beautiful, in their way. Carnivorous, you know.

SLUG:  So... what are you guys, anyway?
Some kind of... vaudevillian divorce... fairies?

Oh, wait. I get it. This *h*-rash, it's connected to unresolved
feelings from the divorce, which have only now manifested,
several years later, and once you guys get involved, fix
things, it'll go away?

SPATZ:  Did you hear that spitz? Isn't he darling?
You're not the sort to have a story like that.

SPITZ:  Bloody primrose idiot.
Do we look like "fairies"?

SLUG:  Well....

SPITZ:  spatz—get your valise.

SLUG:  It's just....
It's
Well, your tuxedos, for one thing. And the tap shoes.
You've got to admit–

SPITZ:  I suppose our size is going to come into this next.

Honestly. Can't see past the petals on the stem, the lot of you.

SPATZ:  We're your crack team of lawyers.

SLUG:  But you're only, what, three inches high?

SPITZ:

SPATZ:

SLUG:

SPITZ:  Three and a half.

SPATZ:  Plus another quarter when we're in the courtroom.

SLUG:  You know, I never hired you.

SPITZ:  Retained.

SLUG:  Fine.... I never "retained" you.

SPITZ & SPATZ:   Details.

### on distinguishing a gentleman out of the rubbish heap of rogues, brash bandicoots, and other undesirables

The most valuable accessory to the contemporary girl's refinement is that special trinket decorating her arm—a companion of suitable breeding. It is fashionable these days to pair with a *gentleman.* A potential suitor's pedigree may appear to be selfevident, but take heed: with the ease and simplicity of current modes of dress and the laxness of modern manners it is increasingly difficult to recognize genuine sophistication with the naked eye. It is nearly effortless for any old popinjay to insinuate himself in polite society, given a deft handshake and an etched calling card. The shrewd girl must navigate advances from such upstart vulgarians, for they will rake through civil circles in abundance. The first thing to note is that a gentleman is not to be mistaken for a fop or a dandy. Elegant, unquestionably, but not garish, selfabsorbed, or pampy. He should not be more physically affable than you, and should not fancy himself such. An escort of solid standing will be quiet, stable, and protective. He will not boast his personal or business affairs, negotiate in a raised voice, or exceed normal parameters in activities such as drinking, betting, or cavorting. He will not take corporal liberties with your person, but will instead comport himself with a crisp and civil detachment from your affections. He may seem merely average upon first glance, less riveting than the peacocks of days gone by, but his stolid grace will reflect your discretion and good taste in the public mirror. Your commitment to a gentleman will bear the mark of suitability that quenches your matrimonial plans with the thrill of adequacy.

consort with an    au courant ruralist    from time to time
slack vowelled charm    captivates
allures    with rustic starched conservationism

disseminates fantastical treatises    on dewdropped
leaf collection    mashed marigold dyes    and
energy derived from electric beetle secretions
attempting to gain mastery    of the wind
and the people's ovation

over pheasant laced chamomile
mustard steamed dilution    hand rustled
sapping unaccustomed throats    attentive

stern notes    strummed saccharine    combating urban decay
mopheaded hypnotism    infesting fatigued ear

pressed petal banality    grates bucolic
yet    he demonstrates remarkable haberdashery
glove dandied peacockery    buttoned and baubled chic
flaunting meticulous notions    pastoral frippery
and a failure to    account

## *schooldays*

well    it was the expectation    that put me off    though it is
i suppose    an ethical matter    for some
but    i know i'm nobody's fresh game
my complaints registered  shards of inattention  sharp  and blunt
absent compliments of saccharine insincerity regarding
surprising maturity
a curiously singular adult sensibility
only hollow breaths    dulled by inevitability    chalkthick air
no pretense    even    to seduction    guess i'm old fashioned that way

met with a palmist        previously
had a startling knack for housekeeping
an astonishing tic     for taut triggery
columns of saucers    towered gleaming   among
zen swished teacups      stacked sinkside


a combination of chiromancy and politesse
leading to watercress sandwiches      ginger pinwheels
hand rolled truffles      dusted with powdered sugar and
scintillating convictions about
the artistry of the palm


creases and wrinkles    curve portentous
whetting handfuls of days     divined dependable
the dermatoglyphics determined    a delightful deficiency
for the espousal    palmar features read plainly
pinky lines lacking    revives prospects unbolted

a doubtful eyebrow     raised in luscious arch
difficult to ignore     but still a possibility     through
razorwire grin     fishlimp handshake
and an unstated third term

melting butterfly cookies     treacle coffee     out of doors

outweighed

competitive listening     collage of sleepy finched phrases
flavouring everything medicinal

### on the fine art of repose

One of the greatest blunders that the inadequately schooled girl can perpetrate is to presume that she must appear active at every moment she is visible within society. On the contrary, my dear girls. Do not kid yourselves that all the efforts of deportment, dressing, primping, and other performances of politesse are not positively ex*haust*ing. One mustn't mistake, however, the opportunity for a properly dignified repose as an excuse to appear lazy or worn out. Indeed, inappropriate inaction can prove socially fatal. During a correct attitude of repose, one must not slump the torso, slouch the shoulders, or allow the knees and feet to fall to the sides, in vulgar posture. Instead, recline the shoulders and torso, ever so slightly, back straight (no sinking into the upholstery!) and feel free to angle the chin slightly to one side or the other. Focus the eyes on some far away point in the room, as if engaged in dreamy contemplation of some detail from an earlier conversation or a snippet of the latest Romance you have perused. The repose, if executed flawlessly, will raise your person in the esteem of any suitor worth his salt, which will in turn, though you scarcely need reminding, be infinitely rewarding to your matrimonial ambitions.

# Butterflied Kidney

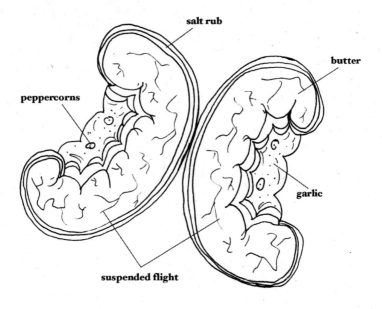

salt rub

butter

peppercorns

garlic

suspended flight

## *mode*

Sever kidneys nearly in half along inner seam     leaving thin
connective membrane
Crook finger under loose skin     peel outer casing back     careful
thin     strips
Discard dermal shreds     or set aside for ribbon garnish
    (renal artery and papilla may be threaded into decorative bow
    for final plating)
Steep in clarified butter     before flashfrying     in sharp cast iron
Turn once renal pyramid achieves crisp sensation     on keen tongues
Splay butterflied kidney over dry sippets
One organ per guest

## *"bumblebee picnic"*
### *featuring the legal stylings of spitz & spatz*

SPITZ: Get your shoulders up. And for peonies' sake, get that chewy out of your slack gob.

SLUG: It's gum.

SPITZ: Whatever it is, it's making you look like a drooping daffodil. That and your atrocious posture. You need to stake that sagging neck of yours.

SPATZ: I knew it wasn't chewy. Smells like blackcurrant and... something else.

SLUG: It's iced blackcurrant with a menthol shell. Care for a piece?

SPATZ: Don't mind if I do.

SPITZ:

SPATZ: Egad, this tastes like....

SLUG: Cough syrup. That's what makes it so good.

SPITZ: Sounds like a pickled herring of an idea. Who would buy that compost?

SLUG: Well no one besides me, I guess. They've discontinued the line. I've got the last case of it in the city.

SPATZ:    Discontinued? Maybe we can have a word with them.
Legal style. On account of your appalling dependency
on the chewbacks. When we're done with all this divorce
palaver, of course.

SPITZ:    Which we won't be if we don't get this tulip
straightened up for the stand. Now. Tell the court about
the first time you noticed when things were curdling over.

SLUG:    I don't know. Who notices things like that?

SPATZ:    That doesn't bode well. You need to tell a good
story. Judges like that. If you could stitch together all
your feelings and swatches of memories into a sweet little
narrative, you'll sway the willows your way.

SLUG:    I guess when she stopped coming home right after
work. That couldn't have been good.

SPITZ:    OK look. We've been real patient up to now. But
you've got to give us something to work with. Really. Not
coming home after work? What kind of stale tripe is that?

SPATZ:    It is a bit on the lean side. Couldn't you throw in
some sleepless nights? Maybe a few bits on the side?

SPITZ:    For either one of you. We can spin it either way.

SLUG:    Well what can I do about it now? It's a fairly standard story, with absolutely no elements of surprise, or charming anecdotes. No great plot points.

SPITZ:   No booze and whore binges for either party?

SLUG:   I wish. But no. Just some pretty regular drifting, wanting different things....

SPATZ:   We'll work something up. How would you feel about a rare illness?

SPITZ:   Or an emotional disability. That's not a tough sell.

SPATZ:   Yeah. What we're looking for is something to play the heartstrings.

SLUG:   Look, I'm telling you flat. Hearts will not be wrenched. Tears will not be jerked. I'm just happy the heartless shrew has moved on to other marks to sink her teeth into.

SPITZ:   That's going to cost you.

SLUG:   Well, snuff it, what–

SPITZ & SPATZ:   Whoa!

SPATZ:   I'll thank you not to sling about with your heckin' and jeckin'.

SPITZ:   Don't think you can slip any of that *if you see Kate* by us, tea leaf, and that's a lock.

SPATZ:   That kind of sasslip is simply not going to glide, with us or on the stand.

SPITZ:   While we're at it, flutter an eye at that slouching. You haven't got a sunflower's chance of pulling this scene off.

SPATZ:   A good support brace could work that out. It's his toxicity I'm concerned about–it's a flutterboard in the rapids. It'll contaminate the judge, the other legal counsel.... The whole room will be polluted with his viscous sludgemouth.

SPITZ:   And have you ever noticed how he babbles like a giddy grasshopper? Not a lick of sense out of him since our retainer.

SPATZ:   We could work on that too. We'd need a more sophisticated brace, but it could be done. A rubdown with a bit of diplomacy.

SPITZ:   But what about that general air of incompetence? We'll need a mighty big net to keep all that hair in.

SPATZ:   You're thinking plan B, aren't you.

SLUG:   I hope plan B is leaving me alone.

SPITZ:    Cut the snapdragon lip, chip. That won't cut the mustardseed with us.

SPATZ:    You won't be in court.

SLUG:    Great.

So listen, thanks for looking over my papers and everything. Nice meeting you, and best of luck. All that.

SPITZ:    What's with the brush, slush? We're not going anywhere.

SPATZ:    Of course not. We wouldn't abandon a client off the cuff like that. We're responsible professionals.

SPITZ:    You ever see a drunk bumblebee?

SLUG:    Is this another one of your cautionary tales?

SPATZ:    Not quite. It's one of his lesson jams.

SPITZ:    Bumblebees, they love picnics, see. And lots of people have beer, White Russians, what have you, with their chicken bones.

SLUG:    And bees drink it?

SPATZ:    Can't get enough of it. You should watch them

sometime–all punch lolling and redeyed. Sweet, really, when you see their beeline degrade into a hazy zigzag.

SPITZ:   Uhem.

Well, the bouncer bees at the hive, they don't like it. No one in the hive is allowed to be a drunkard. Interferes with productivity. So they give them the push off to sober up before coming home. Mostly they sleep it off under the shade of a buttercup. But some of them, they're not used to the liquor, so their thoughts are all bent out of shape. Moan on about their own bed, and whatsuch. They don't take the bounce to heart and try to force their way in. Then the bouncer bees sting them to death. Problem solved.

SLUG:   So... you're going to sting me to death at a picnic?

SPATZ:   No no. We're on your side, remember?

SPITZ:   It's the one chance rule. That's the lesson, primrose. You've blown your chance.

SLUG:   OK... so no more court, right? I can live with that. Gladly.

SPATZ:   Well still more court. Just no more *you* in court.

SPITZ:   We're going to have to go in without you.

SLUG:   Can you do that?

SPATZ:   It's for the best. We won't sabotage you like you will.

SPITZ:   Let's blow this pillow fight. We've got court fables
   to float.
   spatz–

SPATZ:   Valises!

BUTTERFINGERS:


hey chicken cat      grind this through the earfunnel
a squirrel and a grasshopper crack into a saloon
one to the other:     if marriage is
the antidote to corporal fervour
i'm punchpleased to have slipped
the script      down
the sewer grate

### "fits and starts"
#### featuring approximated nonchalant banter

SLUG:   I know what you must be thinking, seeing me up and about this early. Lugging all my sample collection kit bits around. I don't normally get such an early start. Didn't used to, anyway. God, it's just gone five. I haven't slept yet is all. Thought I ought to take some scrapings, since I was up anyway.

It's these *h*'s. They're just... growing in strength and number by legions. Prickling and stinging as they hook-a-crook into my torso. You can't see it from the outside, but I can feel them rooting into the membrane, anchored well below the epidermal surface. Incorrigible. Would you believe I've identified at least seven distinct fonts? I'm sure there are others, but the ones on my back, well, they're tough to make out. Some are nearly illegible, reflected backwards in the mirror. Audacious pests, they're loving every minute of this. There's no way to shuck this rogue typography. They don't even blanch in the face of minty antifungals and strawberry antibacterials. Antimicrobial gel... forget it. Even the grape ones, and they're supposed to be invincible. My prescription for that one had to be signed by two doctors, and nothing. Still overrun by *h*-roots coiling 'round my organs, strangling the viscera with pinch and vigour, snaking through intestinal jungle. A thicket of itch, hissing calligraphic sentience through sweetbread cavity.

## on marking the right dancecard

Begin by ascertaining the most beautiful girl in attendance at whatever soirée you've decided to lay your spade. Once you've found the freshfaced fluttering floret, inhale the sweetness of the perfect plum. Then move swiftly to more realistic orchards. Avoid being too diffuse in your aims. Remember, hedging bets with volume never beats playing the long game with one lucky contender. Find a reasonably attractive piece nattering away about the fawniest fashions or whatsuch. She should be of a light demeanor–a pleasantly naïve chatterbox. Once selected and primed for attachment, make use of all the flimflam contour at your disposal to secure anticipated favours.

was in love   with a      folkstar
from afar
until
stubble scratched cheek    croonsoothed
silted sleep  settled    whistled ballads
heralding apocalyptic paradises
stringed birds  celebrate   rosepetalled crumbling
bureaucratic digits  filed airy    frozen midtwirl
pirouette cynicism    flavoured sultry   palatable


leaving curdled thoughts   bunched      melting clusters
the brain's tongue tied      elastic letters  overstretch     pill threadbare


burdock scented phrases  lipsucked      savoured solid
drained to marble    saliva compressed      rolling cheek to cheek
flexed tip teases      nudges   cat's eye    pockets  into pretty pink

# Pancreas Pettitoes

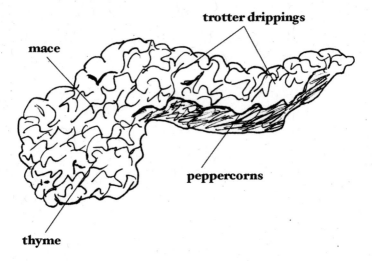

mace

trotter drippings

peppercorns

thyme

## mode

Mince pancreas[1] to a fine pulp
Submerge under a slow and
viscous gravy
Simmer several pairs of hog trotters[2]
in lemonbreezed broth
Split between toes when tender enough
to snap sinew
Set metatarsal oblongs around pooled
pancreas hash for dipping

---

1 Although the coarse, wiry tissue of trotters is generally preferred as a light
snack, they will be an absolute pedal delight on a chilly winter afternoon
when paired with a hearty pulped pancreas.
2 For quick cookery, prepickled or butcher treated parts are the fairy dust
you've been hoping for. Purists, of course, will no doubt prefer to treat
their tender toes of piglets with a solution of hot brine and vinegar prior
to stewing.

## on curbing flirtation

"Will you do me the honour of being my wife?"
The words every girl longs for, naturally. But not so fast!
There's a long and careful road to promenade before securing
such a blissful prospect. First rule to keep under your thumb:
tasteful and reputable behaviour is fundamental. A girl
needn't cheapen herself by giving too much of her person.
Save your generosity, girls, for the food banks and children's
hospitals. A suitor of good breeding ought to know better
than to act in a physically presumptuous manner. However,
gentlemen will be men from time to time. Though she may
be tempted by curiosity, a decent girl will refrain from such
coarse behaviour lest she wind up socially punctured.
A most unsavoury infraction on taste in courtship is the
*French* kiss. *French* or "deep" kissing is far too uncouth with
familiarity to reflect well on refinement. Engagement in
*French* kissing is a gateway flirtation[1] that will certainly lead
a young girl further by whole measures down that slippery
and poorly lit path of unsuitable conduct.

---

1 Other gateway flirtations to mind: the lingering embrace, the vulgar hand-
hold (of the interlaced finger variety), the pouting and/or quivering lip,
and the licentious gaze. For a listing of what lies beyond these seedy gates,
refer to Chapter Six, "A Catalogue of Promiscuity."

i have a sense about    how    these things turn    out
years picked lean    by easy monthly payments
straw bled files    husked skeletal
strewn slapdash    over cracked exertion
the frustration of collection discourse
parasitic accounting incites    lead azide banter
re: granite jawed incompetence

was keen on   an   anaemic prig      once
had distinguished posture    reedy silhouette    swayed humble
arched shoulder pitched forward slender arm crooked brisk at the elbow
angular repose   inviting   gauntbellied admiration

syllables tucked in sinewy cheeks   fortified  vitamin laced confections
bundled tenses   wrapped   concealed hermetic
squirreled tight    to the bone
nimbletongued phrases  loosen    float non sequitur

although

propped centrefocus
disengaged gaze   complements
barely detectable hunch    inclined wrist   hooked finger
calculated detachment    eager for preemptive rejection   unsolicited

was in love with another     cellist     subsequently     had
predictably astonishing hands     slickline willowed     agile graceries
spectacular digitry   flickers   seductive

milk-and-honey     spat     palm centre
pearlescent splatter     squelches over wet knuckles
polished lather     slips     gloves complete
prism bubbles     coast     to     porcelain

settle

burst

evaporate

with beaded water     under     warmed air

## Heart Bundles
*mode*

Assemble gatherings from your intended
suitable items may include:
    fallen eyelashes
    broken nails
    residual kisses
    stale laughter

Wrap together with cheesecloth

Infuse lover's bundle with an appropriate incantation
(anything heartfelt will do)

Fill fluttering organ with bundles and saccharine phrases

Tie off apertures with ribbons of your hair

Save boiling liquid; it makes an ideal love potion
    smacking with a cheeky gastric aftertingle

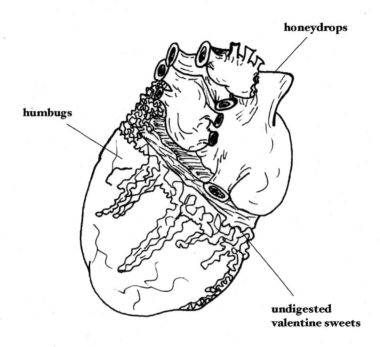

honeydrops

humbugs

undigested
valentine sweets

## "morning moralist"
### featuring a worm's-eye riff

SLUG:   You're not one of those... *people*... are you?
The morning kind?

No, of course not. You wouldn't be.
Have you heard one of them gust lately? A six a.m.
alarm and they think they're entitled to drift through
life with the smarm and selfsatisfaction of assuming that
they're four hours better than the average slob lacking
the kind of clerical job that demands a wake up call at
a *reasonable* hour.

*Oh you haven't lived until you've seen the sun rise every day.*
Bellies full of toast and respectable marmalades. Fingers
stained with inky insolence from gazettes and posts.
Slithery gits.

Early birds... sitting in their sensible midsize cars, smug.
Juicyplump worms writhing between slightly parted teeth,
applying just enough pressure to let the worm know where
he is before he's sucked into shell-pink throat, chased with
a latte and a doughnut, stale, so powdered sugar catches,
slight pressure of expansion before peristalsis ensues.

# HAVE YOU SEEN?

CONTACT 5D IMMEDIATELY:
- SYMPTOM COMPARISON
- OINTMENT EXCHANGE
- h-DATA CATALOGUING
- SYMPATHETIC EAR

*field notes     apartment 5d*
*recorded by slug*
*evidence collected to determine the cause of the h-rash*

SUBJECT 201: common dust balloon


PHYSICAL CHARACTERISTICS
    tumbleweed fluffed     rounded rough
    polyvalent composition:
        wisplight beiges
        sand    fallen food particles
        amputated insect legs    thinveined wings
        sloughed cellular deposits
        and other desiccated dermatology
        flecked red
        bound with stranded hair


BEHAVIOUR
    elusive     withdrawn
    a shrunk violet     introverted in all available corners
    suspected socialite when unobserved     kittenblithe
        with a good sense of humour    and a penchant for
        fine liqueurs
    gestates continuously under heavy furniture
        waiting for victories achieved by population density


RESPONSE TO STIMULI
    soars eager in current of exhalation
    wreaks respiratory havoc in current of inhalation
        engages in alveoli revelry with every breath
    singes in matchlight
    indifferent to action/adventure flicks

vanishes in water      leaving a fine powder of follicle
    remnants

CONTACT WITH *h*'s (IN RASH FORM)
    inflames itching significantly
    incited infection in two of five lowercase helveticas
        promising *h*-irritation
        though has yet to cause new *h*-formations

PRELIMINARY CONCLUSIONS
    observer will succumb to imminent population explosion
        eventually taken down by aggressive cocooning practices
        beginning to burble through the controlling dust
        administration

**AlphabeTics**

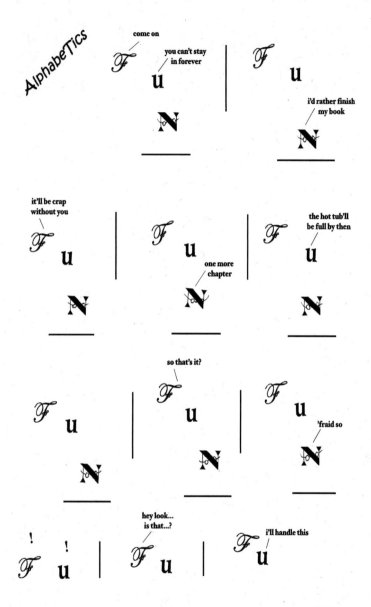

78

# AlphabeTics

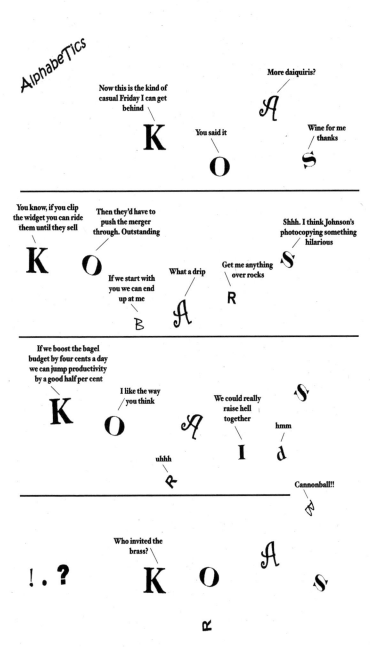

More daiquiris?

𝒜

Now this is the kind of casual Friday I can get behind

**K**

You said it

**O**

Wine for me thanks

**S**

---

You know, if you clip the widget you can ride them until they sell

**K**

Then they'd have to push the merger through. Outstanding

**O**

Shhh. I think Johnson's photocopying something hilarious

**S**

If we start with you we can end up at me

**B**

What a drip

𝒜

Get me anything over rocks

**R**

---

If we boost the bagel budget by four cents a day we can jump productivity by a good half per cent

**K**

I like the way you think

**O**

𝒜

We could really raise hell together

**I**

**S**

hmm

**d**

uhhh

**R**

---

Cannonball!!

**S**

Who invited the brass?

**K**

**O**

𝒜

**S**

**! . ?**

**R**

ALPHABETICS

Z

BACK

RAD

BREEZEBLOCK

Z

---

BLOCK

The Merovingian Script Museum must be around here somewhere.

SAFE

B

*U s u Q*

V

---

PILLOCK

TOAD

I knew we should have stopped for directions.

Just a few more blocks.

A

*U s u Q*

---

LIVERBAY

SLUG

Are you sure it's safe? We should turn back— the children.

Nonsense! We'll miss the exhibit. I've been dying to see how they fit up the ligatures *by hand*.

*Usu Q*

Mummy! Their serif is... pointy.

*U̶ₛᵤ Q*

---

Shhh. Mind your manners, dears. They're just... *common.*

*U̶ₐₛ Q*

---

This whole crowd is barely legible. Must be drugs.

I hear the carpet pages are magnificent.

*U̶ ₐ Qₛ*

---

And the Chelles! Extraordinary.

Just look at them—nibbed with iron gall ink. I suspect they haven't even *seen* a proper quill.

*Q*

*U̶ ₛᵤ*

---

That smell... if you don't get us out of here this instant I'm having you struck-over.

*ₘ Q*

*U̶ ₛᵤ*

Alphabe*Tics*

The Monotype Sort, once roaming all manner of typesetting devices in robust herds, is now among the rarest of the great alphabetic beasts.

This slide, enhanced from a grainy amateur photograph, shows a magnificent specimen, a brawny *b*, at the peak of its vigour. This image remains one of the best modern examples of the beast ever captured by film or net.

specimen 13

Some call it an obsession. A hearty fascination. A bit of fancy run amok. Regardless of how you name it, I stand proud among the Mono game hunters. We are few, but mighty, and will not rest until we've captured, examined, and mounted every elusive husk of monotypography.  Note the flirtatious fanned flourish of the *j*.

specimen 22
(in captivity)

Back when I was a novice, out on my first deep sea expedition, I had a dalliance with a coquettish *b*. Oh, she played coy at first. Batted her symmetry. Fluttered her mechanical florality. Then just as she was about to succumb to my twittering fingertips, she disappeared beneath the surface, lost under the depths of three thousand meters of saline obscurity. Biggest regret of my life.

specimen 26
(artist's rendering)

I once tasted a Monotype *O* that had washed ashore on an unpopulated beach. Sautéed a thin sliver off the tentacle in garlic and olive oil. It was bitter heaven.

specimen 42

## on corporal gluttony

Kiss with your whole body—lovers are gluttons. Begin testing the waters... the fairer sex will most certainly appreciate a delicate touch. The inexperienced kisser may be surprised at the sudden rush of blood from the head at the slightest hint of the impending oscular experience. Not to worry; you'll soon grow accustomed to the light-headedness to which you've fallen victim. Even crave it, yes *crave* it, after a time. And you can be certain that whatever blissful dizziness has beckoned you, your gentle partner will feel it double. Take this opportunity to support her finespun frame with the square of your muscle. Slip an arm about her waist. Draw her in. She'll be grateful for the prop as her knees sway and buckle. She will be convinced to reward your sensitivity. This is the golden moment—tighten the lock on your lips as your bodies gleefully intertwine for that airy tango of embrace.

it has no adequate name        but

    i miss it


        melodic bonecrack
                jointsnap  in
    and out     of place     jubilant expansion puffing
   youthful   decrepitude teases   entices   frayed
edges   cookiecut   stamped out ragged
  muscles stretchached in     need of repair
rethread the skeleton     fresh tissue  elongated
       sinew renewed elastic

fingertips sift     signs of scalpular rupture
        roots tingle blunt digitry     blush fanned fibres
                subtle cracks graze     a stable husk

        epidermal delight     prickles eager palms

push dark curls aside     salted mango wafts     drifts     disperses
        reveals red pucker     a superficial disturbance
                that wants teasing

        keen nail digs
                        worms


                                burrows


                        delectable scales

        petite puncture     widened with a thumb
                        and a scalp fork     finely tuned

        tickle cerebral succulence     dampkissed     sweet
                coo the cerebellum     warble the lobes
                        finfoot for microbial delicacies

        a lick of the pinky  says     you're almost done

consulted with a banker     for a time
scrawled mesmerizing portfolios     ribthick and stacked
pintight     over mahogany     and parchment blotters

exuberant advice threaded     through licksplit bobbins
pitched on filaments  of secured growth
no interest folds     high yields
bubbles and bears     dribbling doe-eyed returns

exhilarating tales unreeled     with alluring velocity
enthralling efficiency
parables of treasures troved     filleted   drained bonedry
wagons fixed by   roguish odds of insolvency

nestegg ventures   shuffled     numerically dazzling fancies
rolled over     speculated plump

romances of futures filed impenetrable
seductive reliability     buoyant with prime rates
pie chart enchantment

### on diversifying your portfolio

Politesse and general female restraint prevents your frittered finches from taking the lead in matters of repertoire. It is, naturally, left to your hat to introduce variety into your performance. Not only will your prowess impress, it is also within your responsibilities to educate in the practice of love as in any matter of importance—current events, athletics, the basic function of simple mechanical devices.... The modern gentleman will vary his stroke with a basic set of four to six different models, more as he gains experience and confidence. It may drag like common drudgery at first, to learn and rehearse your technique. But rest assured; the fellow who wants to reap the benefits of electrifying a stogy smoocher will first read up, then practice his *orbicularis oris* pucker numb. Your languid lovers and your nimbled lips alike will be chuffed ambrosial with your osculatory agility.

*field notes     apartment 5d*
*recorded by slug*
*evidence collected to determine the cause of the h-rash*

SUBJECT 26: spider (behind-refrigerator foundling)


PHYSICAL CHARACTERISTICS

    black fuzzed torso     puffed plump

    abdominally ostentations     garish scarlet streak

    bogstandard eight legs

    optically invested (several of the eyes wink     dramatically

        one does not     dramatically)

    spinnerets intact     apparently functioning

        (evidence of silken biological production)

    booklunged     freshfaced     warm     lively

    demeanor of a Chuck or a Rew

        (refuses to confirm either appellation)


BEHAVIOUR

    bounds toward netted insects

        all hours     but exhibits especial joy for nocturnal snacking

    swift     methodical consumption of prey

        death keen     impatient

    can jump to heights in excess of nine inches

        though generally does not

    weekly tangleweb demolition and reerection

        each more disheveled than the last

        one domestic disgrace after another

RESPONSE TO STIMULI

    displays shrillshrieked resentment of foot wetting

        (wine    water   carbonated liquids)

    suspicious of overseasoned cuisine    rejects most pepperencrusted

        insects

    flouts prompts toward obstacle courses   rodent wheels

                carefully prepared naturewalks

    underappreciative of cut flowers   penny chocolates   gumdrops

        (arthropod arrogance)


CONTACT WITH *h*'s (IN RASH FORM)

    virtually endless capacity for meditative perching on or near

        shoulder *h*'s

    curious preference for serif


PRELIMINARY CONCLUSIONS

    surprisingly affable    social    compassionate

    a generally decent companion

    not plausibly complicit in *h*-contagion

*field notes     apartment 5d*
*recorded by slug*
*evidence collected to determine the cause of the h-rash*

SUBJECT 27: spiderbite


PHYSICAL CHARACTERISTICS
    redbeige    blueing edges
    quartersized    roughly spherical
    deep core lumped hard
    curdled flavour     tastes of vinegar and past due dairy
    pusriddled    tending toward infection


BEHAVIOUR
    dull ache at doublefanged puncture point
    pulsates    slightly audible    to the trained ear
    swells    alarmingly before the eyes
    throbs unprovoked
    predicts unwanted phone calls with a single sharpslivered sear


RESPONSE TO STIMULI
    prickles with hot tea bath
        (green, white, black, and other herbal brews)
    stings during and after light tapping
    festers beneath bandages    gauze    linen wraps
    twinkles at onset of inclement weather
    unresponsive to *h*-salve

CONTACT WITH $h$'s (IN RASH FORM)
>   not visibly relevant

PRELIMINARY CONCLUSIONS
>   medically unthreatening to date
>   potentially requires independent antibiotic treatment

### "of Property"
### featuring the cerebral cartography of spitz & spatz

SPITZ:  You throw like a guppy. All fins. Put some bicep
into it.

SPATZ:  I wish you'd quit with all the sea creature gibes.
You know full well I'm perfectly grounded.

SPITZ:  Of course. In an airy sort of way.

SPATZ:  Even for a clever tux like you that's not fair.

SPITZ:  Right. It's *air.*

SPATZ:  You need a new quipman, spitz. Those mortarballs
you're dropping won't even make it with an iron lung.

SPITZ:  You saying I'm longwinded?

SPATZ:

SPITZ:  Full of hotair?

SPATZ:

SPITZ:  A blowhard?

SPATZ:

SPITZ:  Short of breath?

SPATZ:

SPITZ:   Wheezing? Panting?

SPATZ:

SPITZ:   Asphyxiating?

SPATZ:

SPITZ:   Ah, quit with the clam act and toss again. We've
          got business here.

SPATZ:   You're just sore about the judge. But you know
          Old Man Harrison's never... understood our approach.
          We got real slick tactics, you and me. We slip through
          some people's fingers is all. We're rebels. Courtroom
          insurgents. Mutineers! A pair of legal mavericks, leaving
          a dusty trail of dropped jaws in our wake.

SPITZ:   Half shell the oyster and put some muscle into
          the bean this time.

SPATZ:   Missed again—do you think she felt that? It's just a
          little dried kidneybean, after all. Not terribly inconvenient?

SPITZ:   Hand me that sac of kidneys, spatz. Watch how
          it's done.

SPATZ:   I really don't think you need to wind up like that.

Textbook showoffery, that is.

SPITZ:   Aha! First time out, thank you kindly.

SLUG:   Ow!

BUTTERFINGERS:   what is it?

SLUG:   You've got to be kidding.

BUTTERFINGERS:   just face forward and watch    whatever
it is it'll go away
or quiet down of its own accord   given enough time
and    not enough attention

SPATZ:   Well I can't say I support your methods, spitz,
but they sure do click the strand on the head.

SPITZ:   He's stumbling up the aisle now—grab his collar on
the way by.

SLUG:   Ow! You're pinching my skin. I might've known you
two would be hovering around.

SPATZ:   Lovely to see you again, master slug. Is that your
tomato down there?

SPITZ:   She's a real peach. Not bad at all.

SLUG:   She's not my... tomato. Just a neighbour. A friend.

SPITZ:   Can't take your toxicity, eh, pineneedles? Figures.

SLUG:    Pineneedles? That's a bit rich from you.

SPATZ:   So you like the pictures, huh…. Sure they're all sweet
         and silvery. But these talkies, they really put a clamp on the
         old physical scene. No one ever mentions that these days.

SPITZ:   Now look, you're upsetting spatz.

SPATZ:   Not that it matters much to me. We've always been
         wordmen, you see. But a lot of dear friends have fallen to
         the talkies, I don't mind telling you.
         Still, they're good for courtship, I suppose.

SLUG:    I'm not courting.

SPITZ:   Ah, false hope, then. Delicious.

SLUG:    I'm just taking in a film. And now I'm missing it.

SPATZ:   We've got a report, number one client!

SPITZ:   Some real progress. Tell him spatz.

SPATZ:   The thing is—

SLUG:    Here we go.

SPATZ:  Quite. The thing is, in this... current climate of...
dropped jaw justice—

SPITZ:  We haven't lost. spatz, get ahold of yourself.
You sound like a weeping angelfish.

SPATZ:  No no, we haven't lost. I certainly didn't mean
to imply—

SLUG:  What did I lose?

SPATZ:  You shouldn't think of this as a loss, per se.

SPITZ:  Per nothing. It isn't a loss, just something off the
table. Plus something not lost at all. So there you go.

SLUG:  Fine. What didn't I lose?

SPITZ:  Your monkey cup, she said on the stand today the
only thing she could swallow about you anymore is—

SPATZ:  Well, the only thing you had left she was interested
in, you see—

SPITZ:  Yes. spatz's line of questioning tickles the nostalgia
gill a bit. It's quite astonishing, really. Very impressive how
that waterfall of reminiscence begins to tumble....

SPATZ:  You're too kind, spitz. Honestly, I don't know what it
is—a gift some say. But I'm just being me, at the quick of it.

Just little old spatz from–

SLUG: And little old you lost me…?

SPITZ: Don't be a daisy. We didn't lose you.

SPATZ: Not entirely.

SPITZ: Barely at all.

SPATZ: Only your accent.

SLUG:

SPATZ: When she started in on your first encounter, she mentioned how enchanted she was by your accent.

SLUG: Accent? We're both from the same country.

SPITZ: Different provinces, you plum. She's from Saskatchewan. They talk very different like. So she says.

SPATZ: She got weepy. Fell in love with your regionalism all over again. For a moment.

SPITZ: Then she remembered where we all were. Caught the venom afresh.

SPATZ: It was your eye, glassiness and all, and your *o*, she said.

SPITZ:   We held firm on your eye. That you can take to
the bank.

SLUG:   My I?! But how–

SPATZ:   Now you're getting hysterical. Not leaping to
proper conclusions.

SPITZ:   Think about it... your *eye.*

SPATZ:   Winks and all. But it's your *o* you should be
concerned about. If anything.

SPITZ:   Right. You needn't be concerned about anything.

SPATZ:   No no. Of course not. Nothing at all.

SPITZ:   Nothing. See?

SLUG:   How's that?

SPATZ:   All you've got to do now is make sure you turn over
your accent–*o*'s and all–to the bench by the 30th of this
month, and *voilà*! *C'est fini.* See?

SLUG:

SPITZ:   Don't confuse the turnip. He's really the plain
English sort. Bottom line, primrose, you've got 21 days to
turn over your accent.

SPATZ:  But we're holding tight to the fight for the aquarium. You may still get that. And some other bits and bobs.

SLUG:  But how? How does this work? The accent bit.

SPATZ:  Well, it's not my place, but if pressed, I'd say a nice box. Something in a natural wood, I should think. Maybe beveled. Smart but not ornate. Dignified.

SLUG:  No, I mean how can something like this happen at all? How could you put something like a person's accent–

SPITZ:  On the table. Yes. We, strictly speaking, didn't. Your venus flytrap did.

SLUG:  But surely you can see that this is… absurd?

SPATZ:  Irrelevant. It's a court order.

SLUG:  But it's not like the house. The cars. The dog, even…. It's… part of me. Part of my being.

SPATZ:  Isn't he precious, spitz? You're having a crisis of grammar, chuck. You see, divorces are about property. And that means you have to give up some of the things you thought were yours, singular, but through a series of documents and intentions became yours, plural. Only now you've got to get back to yours, singular. Or in this case, hers.

SLUG:

SPITZ: They never get the philosophy of it.

SPATZ: Yes. spitz is a real philosopher. But sometimes people–the less philosophically minded–don't quite... follow his cerebral cartography.

SPITZ: I knew it would get around to being my fault eventually.

SPATZ: It's not anyone's fault. Except the less philosophically minded. Like Old Man Harrison. And the opposing counsel. It is a bit on their shoulders.

SPITZ: But philosophy isn't a shortcoming.

SPATZ: Of course not. There, there. It's a very sophisticated style of questioning. Master slug–run an index over his spine... nothing like friendly digitry to dam the tears.

SPITZ: "He that is nourished by the Acorns he pickt up under an Oak, or the Apples he gathered from the Trees in the Wood, has certainly appropriated them to himself. No Body can deny but the nourishment is his. I ask then, when did they begin to be his? When he digested? Or when he eat? Or when he boiled? Or when he brought them home? Or when he pickt them up?"

SPATZ: Hand me your handkerchief. spitz is at his

finest with Mill.

SPITZ: Locke.

SPATZ: Are you sure? It smacks of Mill to my ear.

SPITZ: I think you'll find it's Locke. I'd never bring Mill into this. Never.

SPATZ: Yes yes, I quite agree. Far too delicate to be dragging Mill about whipwhap. Times like these.

SLUG: Apples and acorns? This has nothing to do with me.

SPITZ: Oh no no.

SPATZ: I'm afraid I'm with spitz on this one. It has everything to do with you.

SPITZ: Everything.

SLUG: Like....

SPITZ: OK. Say you eat an apple.

SPATZ: Or an acorn.

SPITZ: Yes. This is a time for precision. An apple or an acorn. Say you eat one of those. Then it becomes your *property.* See? On account of all the peristalsis and whatsuch.

SLUG:

SPITZ:   Listen primrose, haven't you gone about gathering
words your whole life? Boiling them? Digesting them?
Whatever?

SLUG:    I really don't see–

SPATZ:   Shush. He's gathering his glide.

SPITZ:   Well, you've put your labour into them, forming
them with your larynx and lips and tongue…. Putting in
the effort and work to mould them in your own mouth.
With that labour, they've become your property.

SPATZ:   And the real genius of spitz's logic here, the real
genius of it, is that your assets have been increased
astronomically. All your body processes are *property*,
when you think about it.

SPITZ:   I'd option some that bile you're carrying around,
if only they'd approve our petition to list it on the open
market.

SLUG:    This is an outrage! You went through all that
"philosophy" to declare parts of my person as property only
to lose them in the settlement? I'd fire you if I'd actually
hired you in the first place.

SPATZ:   Retained.

SPITZ:   You know, spatz, I'm starting to think this sweet potato isn't grateful for our efforts.

SPATZ:   It certainly seems so.

SPITZ:   Time was a fellow appreciated his representation.

SPATZ:   Wined and dined the eagles. Oh yes. Sky was the limit, to my mind.

SPITZ:   It's getting a bit lean on gratitude in here, wouldn't you say, spatz?

SPITZ & SPATZ:   Gather the valises!

## on the electric lip[1]

A surefire kink to tuck in your osculatory arsenal is the *electric lip*. All the rage at the current trend in kissing parties, it will turn your pretty poppy into a spirited spark plug. Begin by hypnotizing her with your nimble footwork across the carpet, then just as the applause begins to clack syncopated adoration, lean in for a peck square on that sweetly supple rosebud. And FLASH! The blue spark of your electrified lips will mesmerize her into your service. The physical flicker will be the first layer of tantalizing your twinkling tulip, but it will be the glimmer of your snapdragon labiate skill that dazzles everlastingly. It needn't challenge the confidence of us gents that it is merely static electricity, not the ethereal bond between you and she, generating the pleasurable buzz of your mutual lipshock.

---

1 For best results, reserve attempts at the electric lip for treading upon carpeted areas, in the dryer weather.

## *"the bibliotheca of bygone beaux"*
### *featuring syllable sifting by butterfingers*

all downhill


slippery


a *parisienne* potato
(cute as a cueball  and just as obnoxious)
all your beetons and barbs   billowing up
blowing in the palm of your      handsomely assholic   dustjackets
quotations parsed     for distinguished exaggerations


those colours   darling   fail to detonate
sonnet stench infiltrating the sheets    sitting around  in a pool  of
your own
lexical narcissism     parafinned hand stroking   blunt chin
held at considered angle     to achieve greatest effect
as yet   humbug   no available treatment
for the poetically incontinent

freon fingerchill     snaps vertebrae   brittle   unsuspecting
so cuff up your sleeves     don your best lycra and satin
and we'll to the wolves with it


fingers latexed       scalpel on hairtrigger
volumes of verse     laid out flat    unwrapped spines cracked   *écorché*
vivisection  preferred     anaesthesia optional
sentences flayed    gutted skillfully   layer upon layer of sinew exposed
inked veins tendril  from the touch      titillating coyness
vital fluids suctioned    with appropriate care and method
efficient sterilization
a matter of hygiene   (hands kept free of smearing-contagion)
but also convenient for peering

BUTTERFINGERS:


                    hey chicken cat        crunch this cartridge
                       into the hobobrunch slurry


          a little fescennine        between a couple of feckless follies
   one to the other:    a crisp kingfisher to
                       bag the bromide bride    with the run mascara
                    bilk the twill dove     score a triple of cherries
                    then slot it all    through the tympanic lobe
                          chop the mop      and scatter

### *on springing the snare with flair*

A pedigree gentleman will not trip so easily onto the hook. As the appropriate strain of flirtation is essential, reserved charm will strike just the right key to pierce his veneer of social conduct. An ocular gesture will wink volumes above an itinerant hand any day. Given that gentlemen expect to hold the position of dignified pillars in their sweetpeas' affairs it will be most effective to partially fill the ducts promptly before entering his company. A few rapid blinks will present the most satisfying dewyeyed shimmer. Dreaminess of this sort is invariably a flutter in the right direction.

# S-SQUARED BARRISTERS AND SOLICITORS

**Re: Loveletters, an Interoffice Declaration of Highest Importance**

Dear spatz:

Further to your initial declaration (enclosed), I have no choice
but to respond, darling hayseed, with a solid octagon, crisp and
scarlet. I advise you to sweetstep the slick, chum. All swirl
and flush, flutter. Peacock pageantry and tangled cartography.
Cue emotional piano 02.

Sincerely,
spitz
encl.

*trust your legal snarls to our white-gloved hands*

# 𝒮𝒮 S-SQUARED BARRISTERS AND SOLICITORS

litigation compound A • corner davenport • veer left at the silk hibiscus ☎ we'll call you

**Re: Loveletters, an Interoffice Declaration of Highest Importance**

Dear spitz:

Oh, my little vaudevillian vagabond. Fritterbunch. My honeylipped tartlet, scented earlgrey circulation. Limelit at your cherryblock work tablet across the davenport. Affection is a crooked bowl.

Humbly Yours,

spatz

*truſt your legal snarls to our white-gloved hands*

SLUG: You're hobbled! What happened?

BUTTERFINGERS:                               inflamed joint   stretches defunct
            frayed   pulsed ragged   inert elevation
        coddles the swell   kindles vertical dysfunction

SLUG: You can't even see the patella anymore. It's all... spongy.

BUTTERFINGERS:                       spiderbodied beasts burble visible
            plum capers and crescents   seethe   fidget
        arachnoid  frolic  flourishes     under translucent bruises
        impatient for pinprick drainage   savouring recovery

SLUG: Your wordrash... it's getting kinetic? Or, no, you've always
    been clumsy haven't you. Not a new symptom then.
    That's some beauty crack you've got there. So what, you fall
    off your wire?

BUTTERFINGERS:

## *"reception"*
### *featuring a highwire with several linguistic misadventures*

        everything rests on a sharp toe   chalked dusty white
                    sturdy pliability cloudsoftened
                leatherwrapped   in pinkblush
            elegant assurance   ribbonned tight   to the calf
    surefoot slides to a leap   pivot into   wellplotted tumble
    plucky flipped poise   sags braided wire   centred netless
                    hovering amid

*teacakes with currants    thank you    raisins are so    dated        guffaw*

primposed feasters    ravish the décor    and haughty bridal banter
intense debates over frills and hoops    baby's breath ringlets
pinned lilies    pearls bustled neatly    into chiffon

*but that parasol  and glove maneuver        how unsettlingly quaint*

snip

snap

*and that rosebud gloss    well    a girl really needs to be    seamless    to pull*

snip

*making the rounds  i see    my    don't you look radiant    dear*

*just wait 'til the moon starts honey that rosebud won't stay glossed for long*

snap

ounces of fun    viewed tightrope high
betties and babes    set against silver    lacy streamed cloth
cookieblonde and pinkbowed with    the insistence of
ceremony and  circumstance    contractually obliged devotion
mutoscoped in full colour    buzzed with twitterchatter soundtrack
fixes longing for the return of the
coin-in-the-slot peepshow business    a fit alternative
considering silence    before a second trip across the wire

*can't believe little eliot's going to be five now     seems like yesterday*
*it was our turn    to take a spin   on the newlywed granite*

slackline twirl    finished with hand flourish
spun subtlety   floats the line   meticulous

but   stray words   litter the wire chaotic
having drifted upward   from
nets of pampy headed natters   competitive storytelling edged
pungent   with tart braggery
extolling achievements in the field of
gestation   foetuses planted   watered   ripened
to perfection   instigating parental smugness
and assumptions about the neighbours

snip

*i don't see joanie as the marrying kind    sharp shoulderpadded walk*
*blunt haircut   she'd be better in business   shame though   if you ask me*

snap

snip

freehand flexibility   glides   flicks quickfooted moxy
angular velocity   roots pivotpoint ankle
shifts to regal wristed perch
airy biomechanics   trip seasoned acrobatics
invert the banquet palatable   relief of fleeting tolerance

dialogue balloons tumbled   haphazard
upturned tact surfaces    swerve a wandering   *blunt* and *business*
hanging behind disrupted  foot
flip    twist    roundoff   stuck landing
posture recovered fluently    in spite of prattlechat disturbance

*at this stage of the game    chief    it's all about the numbers pitch*
*crunch the corner office    for fasthanded perks    and other secretarial*
*assistance*

snip

freedom of height    and inversion   comforts
settles    excites    the stomach
fervently swum butterfish    reeling gastric choreography
paired with velvetwinged    insects   decocooned
rollicking the belly elated
ingrained wire impressions    kiss the arch fresh
imprint the fingers    wrap the wrist assertive

snap

until firmfoot meets taut line
impacts    fails to connect    solid
slip of the heel    on  inflexible splinters
littered linguistic fragments pierce leather sole    and skin

snip

snowflake freefall

lightlung gasp    pleasure tightens diaphragmatic
blissful awakening    run through slackened musculature

flip

twist

drift midair    slow waft    coast
to marble floor
*snap*

*well this certainly knocks the fun out of the funambulist*
*writhing on the floor like    that*

audible strain    twitches kneecap    angular rupture rests    repulsive
tendons stretched blue
reddened joints    bubble    swell    fluidfill

*someone had better go comfort the bride*
*biggest day of her life    a shambles*

snip

snap

*imagine    hiring circusfolk    for the big day    cutrate entertainment*
*gaudy enchantment    common and kitsch*

*look    a phoneme lodged in her foot    disgusting*

hand drawn to smarting heel
caresses sharp ache     fingers seek unusual pressures
points of entry    and inflammation

foot raised to the eye
for inspection     probe throbbing puncture
a curious pinky   worms in   amplifies the abrasion
tweezes splinters     determined
unsuccessful

heel raised to ˊ firm lips puckered confident
to suck syllabic poison     freshen the wound
vacuumed shards emerge on the tongue
sharp edges tease     fragile palate
scratch     scrape     nick     soft flesh

extractions coiled inside the cheek     tapered end caught
between thumb and index
detached phrases     strung together
tapeworm long     segmented
pulled carefully through parted lips
stray vocables     desiccated dinnerguest chatter
caught on the wire     perforate     gouge     penetrate
requiring disengagement from the tear
a remnant *k*   still piercing   the heel

SLUG:

### *field notes     apartment 5d*
### *recorded by slug*
### *evidence collected to determine the cause of the h-rash*

SUBJECT 485: butterfingers

PHYSICAL CHARACTERISTICS
    crisp eyed    bookishly magnetic
    avian light    delicate corporal precision    defined  but frenetic
    curiously awkward grace    gawky pointed toe elegance
        floats gossamer over highwire and hardwood
        sweetened by a-line swish
    ambrosial cottoncandy hair    sleekly flipped at ends
        frames blythe blushed cheeks


BEHAVIOUR
    moderately social
        (though socially nimble    despite misanthropic tendencies)
    hums while steeping tea
    favours mismatched porcelain tea bowls
    actively avoids newspapers
        citing disappointment in newsprint texture and sparse copy
    enjoys erratic housekeeping practices
        (strewn books and papers make a preferred décor choice)


RESPONSE TO STIMULI
    hedges on visual contact with *h*'s
    ignores repeated requests for surveys on various contagions
        (instead accuses observer of obsessive *h*-tendencies)
    resistant to    pampyhaired clanceys    organized sports
        modish cocktails    hipster trash
        (to the relief of observer)

answers telephone bell eight of ten times on average
    (audible reluctance for calls occurring in quick succession)
places ample bets at the ponies    given the right slip
squelches inappropriate comments and invasions of personal space
discloses past liaisons with prickling precision
    (in seamless streaming detail    equally upon request
    and unsolicited)


CONTACT WITH *h*'s (IN RASH FORM)
    nil


PRELIMINARY CONCLUSIONS
    a durable rapport
        verging on common courtship    after *h*-recovery

## *an ill cut motto*

but     since you've asked     i do
a little     i'm generally
susceptible to     the congenitally peevish

nerves threaded     tripwire taut     prickly
bashful irritability     perched surly
cliffedged     readied     all
the radical potential of
a perpetual skepticism machine
fingertip sensitive     trimmed tempting

### on the sleeping beauty

Keep it subtle–her head will be filled with enchanted gardens where flirtation is anchored in innocence and anticipation, where beauties are awakened from poisonous slumbers; frogs are turned to princes; witches are discovered and dispatched, all with a petalsilk lip. The perfectly delicate buccal press is your passkey to more rewarding cyssan adventures. Once you've awakened your princess with your best somnolent smooch, comment on her sleepy charm, tease her tousled tendrils, suggest more interesting ways to alleviate the ennui of the gathering morning.

# A Lover's Feast

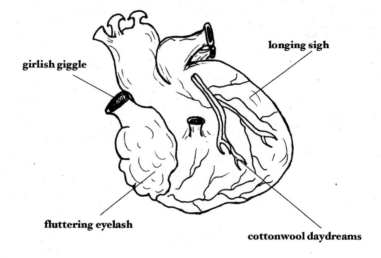

girlish giggle

longing sigh

fluttering eyelash

cottonwool daydreams

## mode

Warm plump hearts between palms[1]
Dredge in flour and tenderness to stop
bleeding
Cauterize any persistently seeping wounds
with a kiss
Prick your finger[2]
Infuse each organ with several drops
of your blood
Roast in lilac-scented broth and birdsongs[3]
Garnish with parsley and a lilt
of your best laugh

---

[1] Freshness counts, dear chefs! Select organs that last beat within twelve
hours of your butcher's harvest.

[2] Thorns of roses given in courtship make the best swords for pricked finger
cookery. However, in a pinch one may also trust a sharp hairpin or the
tip of a paring knife, as long as she remembers to sweeten the steel with
honey prior to stabbing.

[3] Hum lightly to your cardiac treats during preparation for the oven. A happy
heart will bake all the sweeter. The clever girl may also recite a sonnet or
romantic lyric, though do take care to choose wisely; it would be a culinary
travesty to roast in any hint of the unrequited.

**Re: Pulmonary Effusions**

Dear spitz:

A little fish in your ear, my pitterpatter chirpchin. You put
the swish in the trench. The holly in the hock. The tea in the
bone.
You honeycomb my internals. Suck holes in my heart dry,
wishbone the ventricles. Flute the valves sweet.

Fortify your lumps!
spatz

*trust your legal snarls to our white-gloved hands*

# ✍️ S-SQUARED BARRISTERS AND SOLICITORS

litigation compound A • corner davenport • veer left at the silk hibiscus ☎ we'll call you

**Re: Loveletters and Pulmonary Effusions, the cessation of**

spatz:

Cram the mackerel, spindleshanks. Your fatwrapped ticker is strangled in transes and rich cream. Damp the potted pansies. Can the chuckles. And flip (the electricity switch) off.

Drop the chop,
spitz

*trust your legal snarls to our white-gloved hands*

**Re: Cardiac Lava**

Dear spitz:

I implore you for more of your sassy verbiage! Grant me a
twiddle, a twaddle, a dash of wince. You season the pot *prunus
cerasus,* my snaggletoothed vinegar eel! Hit me with more
of your sour, puss. Milkcurdled whisperwords. Your acerbic
linguistic bonbons explode periodontal bliss on my tied tongue.

With bowler in hand,
spatz

*truſt your legal snarls to our white-gloved hands*

# S-SQUARED BARRISTERS AND SOLICITORS

litigation compound A • corner davenport • veer left at the silk hibiscus ☎ we'll call you

**Re: Another Day, Another Brick**

Dear spatz:

Hold the pickle, you charliehaired Clancy. Lay off the
slimstringed lexical mandicant act. It's all holloweared
menacery, whinge and whinny.
Word to the wise, drop a wormwood balm at the whisper
gallery.

You're it,
spitz

*trust your legal snarls to our white-gloved hands*

127

# Tied Tongue

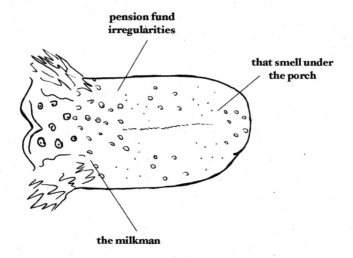

pension fund
irregularities

that smell under
the porch

the milkman

*the tune of the old country ox:*
*best of the looselipped rakes*
*giddily spilled secrets over*
*blonde ale and barley cakes*
*until his farmer's wife heard*
*her own overspiced mistakes*
*simmered to saucy little verbals*
*ladled over pub steaks*

## *mode*

When ripping the tongue from a deserving animal
be sure to reach all the way into the oropharynx,
plucking firmly from the radix.
Uncoil the muscle preparing for a salty soak.
Rub the corpus with a mixture of dried herbs;
tack apex to dorsal with cloves.
Lay in refrigerated spice bath for ten days,
turning tongue once each morning.
During the resting period, you may whisper
desired dinner conversation for turgid
tongue absorption.
Boil seasoned musculature until base bones
give, sliding out of flesh under easy pressure.
Skewer to retain shape while skinning.
Detach savoury muscle from root to extract
remaining gristle webbing and small bones.
Serves one well, or a small party if sliced
thinly into mushroom caps.

slick bristles     glide   molardeep
sweep alert gums   pinked eager       tingled to attention

gentled circles trace    floating thoughts
wafted cosmonauts    thicklimbed    balletic
spontaneous choreography    spins electric
drifts      to visceralled cartographies
of budded muscle  mintstung        and other inner places

mince of squashes    perfumed
sits    in gentle bubbled waiting
jaunty nutmeg trifles    garlic mince    chives    cayenne

a pansied petal to float the surface
retinal gratification    quivering the bud

soup   finely spun   simmering coquetry
gastroflirtation delights        until
boisteroused ginger wrestles    bullies the tongue brash

## "curtain morals"
### featuring a minty oral rinse

SLUG:    An immune system disgrace, and I'm left holding the bag of bones. Reduced to living under the husk of parasite-infested bark. And all he cares about is how often I pop fluoride tabs and stain for plaque. Sweep my gums molardeep.

I thought he'd be a comrade in fighting the impossible decay of the body. But, oh, he's too busy to talk dermatology. He wasn't trained for that. He's got to get down to the brass tacks of pink gingiva. How I'm an overzealous brusher and a delinquent flosser.

Tongue clacked questions about the frequency of flossing lead to judgments of character and moral fibre. *A cavity? Why you must be hanging out in opium dens, son. That's gonna cost you, times thirty two.*

Shrivelled to skulking out of that oversized chair, oral foibles in tow, dribbling complicated mouthwashes from quavering chins. Their eyes filled with the contempt and smugness of dentistry. White coats and Saint Apollonia. The mystique of the dental superhero. Out battling for the public good, waging wars against invisible disease and plaquecreatures. Drafting us all to do our part armed with horsehair bristles on sticks. But really, the best defense they've come up with in hundreds of years of their dental infantry is a piece of guiltstring.

## on the dependable Debbie

It's no secret that the *dependable Debbie* is widely regarded by common male opinion as one of the most banal kisses, practiced only by outmoded cadavers who haven't learned any of our more modern, exciting oral fops and fancies. Why, you cry out, fall back on the thinlipped, closed square smooch when even such a starchy kiss demands intense muscular skill? Surely you think it better to make your move with verve and flair, especially when any prissy pucker demands the same precise coordination of thirty four to thirty six muscles. While it may be a sound viewpoint if a gent fails to astonish his ladyfriends with variation, subjecting them (and himself!) to one dependable kiss after another, be mindful of the situations that invariably call for tried and true lipwork. We've all encountered our share of Skittish Scarlets and Stable Mables, on the brink of twittering away from a perfectly pleasant snog, waxing neurotic on protocol and feminine conduct. Unless you want permanently to frighten away your fare, you'll learn to draw upon the *Deb* as necessary. Think of it as an emergency ace tucked at the ready in your cheek. Periodically send your snooperscope into the hearts and minds of your marks; if you sense discomfort with your artistry, fall back on a moment or two of the sweet, levelheaded *Deb*. This will acquaint your Jittery Jen with your sensitivity and deportment. It will earn her trust and comfort. From convincing demonstrations of banal gentility, it's a short stride to liberate your snogging to the greatest heights of maxillofacial acrobatics.

### "bowler in hand"
### featuring the complimentary closings of spitz & spatz
###    by special request

A morning glory for your lapel,
spatz

A fistful of squashed beetles,
spitz

Like a dragonfly to your fingerperch,
spatz

Splatter your squidinked morsels,
spitz

Like a pinned butterfly,
spatz

Put a clamp on your faucets,
spitz

Enchant your cricks!
spatz

*spitz: That one's corked. Try again.*

Quilling your swish daisy,
spatz

*spitz: That's the spirit.*

Release the Pacinian corpuscle!
spatz

Drawing a pinene bath for your mouthmarbles,
spitz

*spatz: Inspired.*

Winterwash the wordcrust,
spitz

Melting at the tip of your brogue,
spatz

Peppering your winceword,
spitz

*spatz: Raw-bantered beauty. Exquisite.*

Uncoil the packthread,
spatz

Ammonia-soak your tongue depressor,
spitz

Whisperfishes tucked in my humble cheek,
spatz

Pine needles to your flailing gums,
spitz

You're the epoxy of my mismatched valves,
spatz

## Stomach Butterflies
*mode*

Trim attached intestinal and other peripheral tubes,
careful to preserve lower inch of esophagus[1]
Through esophageal opening funnel
twenty-seven to thirty-two plump butterflies[2]
(any vigorous, seasonable variety will answer well)
Steam until visible fluttering dulls to a periodic pulse
Cut and portion tableside for most spectacular presentation[3]

---

1 Not only is the succulent membrane of the stomach delicious, it makes a
practical and tasty cooking vessel.
2 Farmed butterflies are perfectly reliable in a pinch, but freshly caught game
will add indescribable splendour to glisten your plate.
3 If prepared correctly, butterflies should rush out of the cavity upon piercing,
circle the table, and spiral to a finale, resting upon available place settings,
or ornamenting napkin rings for an après-feast sweet.

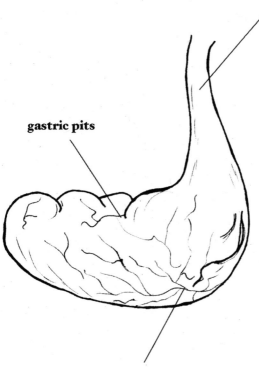

butterfly aperture

gastric pits

lard infusion

### *"a new frog for a reluctant throat"*
### *featuring the buzz and swim of sallow peanuts*

SPATZ:    You'll have to do something about that *r*.

SPITZ:    Make it roll. Trip off that tuliptongue of yours
ricketyrack, like.

SLUG:    Isn't there anything else we can do?

SPATZ:    We could go back to the Bavarian. You had some
good moments with your *ü*. A little spick and span on the
long vowels and you'll not be too far from a new frog in
your throat.

SLUG:    No, I mean isn't there anything we can do to keep
my regular voice.

SPITZ:    Now hold on a minute. You better cut that talk
out kickshaw keen.

SLUG:    It doesn't seem right somehow, to give up my voice
smicksnap like this.

SPITZ:    One, it's not your *voice*. It's merely an accent.

SPATZ:    Too true. An accent is inconsequential to the voice.

SLUG:    What, like metaphorically? Whatever. I'm still–

SPITZ:    Metaphorically. Metaphysically. Ontologically.
Phenomenologically. Biologically. Chemically....

SPATZ:   Biochemically.

SPITZ:   Yes. I knew I was missing something.
   Let's begin with the voice as the essence of your being.

SPATZ:   Window to your soul.

SLUG:   I thought that was supposed to be the eyes.

SPATZ:   The indignation!
   The ear trumpet to the soul, then.

SPITZ:   All your internal... thoughts–such as they are–
   comprise your voice.

SPATZ:   Your voice is, at base, the *you* of the matter.

SPITZ:   The real beauty of what the opposition claimed here
   is that they didn't think of that. If they had we'd be swirled
   down the drain. But they didn't. A magical semantic
   oversight.

SPATZ:   Plus the voice is constructed of sounds made by
   or with the vocal organs, don't forget.

SPITZ:   The rumble and tickle of vibrations in the throat.

SPATZ:   The buzz and swim of bellywaves and syllable
   seedlings.

SPITZ:   The voice is physical. We firmly oppose vivisection.

SPATZ:   On moral grounds.

SPITZ:   And professional. Word like that gets out, suddenly you've got clients ringing your bell at all hours, dropping cases, settling out of court.... Bad for business all 'round.

SPATZ:   You'll still be able to hum and drone along.

SPITZ:   God knows you're going to be able to whinge on and on about it long after the hand-off.

SPATZ:   You just won't inflect as you're used to, is all.

SPITZ:   And two, we've had our best loophole man on the case since it went on the table.
Bloody outrageous, this primrose.

SLUG:   A loophole man? What did he come up with?

SPATZ:   Well this particular cloth is of an especially tight weave, as it were. I haven't found much, I'm afraid.

SLUG:   You're the loophole man?

SPITZ:   Small boutique firm like ours, we've all got to pull together.

SPATZ:   Do our part.

SPITZ: Economize.

SPATZ: Multitask.

SLUG: And you've still got nothing?

SPITZ: Would you look at this spatz? This primrose just sitting around, wallowing in buckets of his own–

SPATZ: Failure. Yes. You really ought to work through this negativity, you know, slug. Not good for the liver.

SPITZ: Or your complexion. Must be why you smell... off.

SLUG: I do not smell. I itch. And I'm looking into that, for the last time.

SPATZ: Now now, calm it down. Corners. Both of you.

SLUG: Couldn't you at least get her to take half of the *h*?

SPITZ: Doesn't work like that.

SPATZ: Besides, you should hang on to it. Could be useful.

SLUG: Useful?

SPITZ: For tax purposes, you plum.

SPATZ: Leave it with us. We'll have it written off quicksplit.

In the meantime, why not wrap your tonsils around
something romantic.... A mid-forties union boss?

SPITZ:   Say "shoit."

SLUG:    Shirt.

SPITZ:   Unacceptable.
This clipped carnation could never be Pinkerton enough
to sling that pinstriped Chicago dressing.

SPATZ:   I don't know.... He brings a certain flailing charm.

SPITZ:   It would be a professional embarrassment to let him
go around garbling sallow peanuts like that.

SPATZ:   Is it the way he washes the anachronism?
The misplaced regionalism?

SPITZ:   Yeah. All that. And more.

SPATZ:   Why don't we try a straight ahead Dubliner?
He could pull something marvelous with that.

SPITZ:   Well someone could. He's a bit rough around the
edges, but with some enthusiasm the primrose may be able
to make a passable emerald brogue.

SPATZ:   It did wonders for Joyce.

Would you like that? A little Joyce to run through
the larynx?

SLUG:   I'm not playing Irish.

SPITZ:   Not generic Irish per se. What about playing Beckett?
  Anyone ought to be honoured.

SLUG:

SPATZ:   The thing to do now is to recognize the inevitability
  of the situation.

SPITZ:   Capitalize on it. It's a cherry of an opportunity for
  the right throat to relish.

SPATZ:   We could really get a character together for you.
  A little twist of the monkey wrench.
  How do you feel about changing your haircolour?

SPITZ:   Or the eyes. That brown is so... wrong for the part.

SLUG:   This is too much. Now I've got to have a whole new
  character?

SPATZ:   Well, to fit the new bill, you see. But uncrease that
  brow–it shouldn't flatten your max. Some homework and
  green vegetables....

SPITZ:   A little grease behind the joint.

SPATZ:   Let's put it in the maybe file for now. Think it over with tea.

Now repeat:

SPITZ & SPATZ:   Earl Grey, Lady Grey, Elephant Grey, Servant Grey
Earl Grey....

## Liver Silk

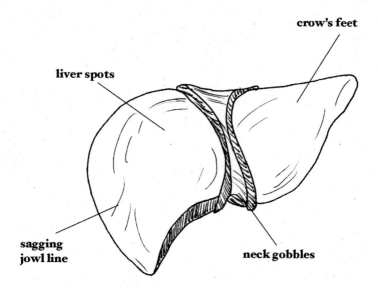

crow's feet

liver spots

sagging
jowl line

neck gobbles

## *mode*

Pulp fatty tissue[1] with a large mortar and pestle
Fold in gelatin blocks to emulsify
Whip into an airy mousse
Refrigerate in jelly moulds[2]

---

1 For a princess satin complexion, smooth one creamy portion over face
and neck nightly. With regular use, your skin will gain a dazzling organic
sheen, making you the belle of the Liver Ball.
2 Liver may also be desiccated for use as protein rich bath crystals. Watch
your petty anxieties waft away, carried on the fluffy scent of Liver Silk!

## on making the most of noncommunicable illness

Prime your bedside visits with flowers, bonbons, or like
sentiment cementing trifles. Your sweetpea will want to feel
the thrill of materiality, particularly at her time of infirmity.
The fairer sex equates trinkets with your tenderness, and as
such, bibbles and baubles prompt her fond recollection of
your affections between calls. While it may seem tiresome
to play nursemaid, consider the romantic currency of
performing the prancing prince to her wilted lily. Take the
honey-eyed appeal of the scene: your faded filly laid out on
her fainting sofa or with any luck, in her own bed, draped
in crisp linens and silk. Loose tresses coiling her sallow
neck. The rush of flushed cheeks painting your ailing poppet
a pretty pale pink. Once you've chatted your dwindling
daffodil into the warm and trusting grip of consolation and
convalescence you may feel secure in advancing. A light strike
with the enticement of pressed lips to feverish forehead will
certainly quiet any quivering doubts and seal her ardour.
From the forehead, think how easily and naturally a lip may
drift over the nose toward a sweetheart mouth, for a long and
breathless buss to flood the mercury under her tongue.

### "parcel post"
### not featuring proper surgery by spitz & spatz

SPATZ:   How about this one? It's simply exquisite, don't you think? Plain, with just a hint of flair at the hinge.

SLUG:   I don't know. Maybe a tin one?

SPATZ:   Tin! Wood's much warmer.

SLUG:   What do I care? Look where it's going.

SPATZ:   Still, though. It *is* your accent. You want it to be comfortable. How do you feel about goldleaf?

SLUG:   Stainless steel?

SPITZ:   The tulip's got a point. It's a perfectly clear and practical metal. Surgeons use it, you know.

SLUG:   Yeah, about that. I still don't see how it's done. It's not... surgical. Is it?

SPITZ:   Do we look like surgeons?

SLUG:   You don't look like lawyers.

SPITZ:   Watch it, taproot.

SPATZ:   It's not properly surgical. Just inevitable. We've discussed that, remember?

SLUG:   Yeah, but. How?

SPATZ:   Once we find a suitable box for it, it's just a tick and a bob through the tongue. A tickle on the bud. Nip of the lip. And that's that.

SLUG:

SPITZ:   You open your trap, see, and while it's loosened into the air–

SPATZ:   In a state of transmission, as it were–

SPITZ:   We flip it in the box, and

SPITZ & SPATZ:   Snap!

SPATZ:   Then stickstuck it's parcel post to Saskatchewan.

*field notes    apartment 5d*
*recorded by slug*
*evidence collected to determine the cause of the h-rash*

SUBJECT 640: household molasses

PHYSICAL CHARACTERISTICS

    sticky    viscous

    congealed a predictable glossy auburn

        but carries curious depth    a black hole quality

    dominant sweet strain    sour undercurrent

        rife with third boiling fortified mineral content

        (nutritionally condescending)


BEHAVIOUR

    slow running    of course

    remains aloof in beaker containment

    pools playing card thin    upon beaker release

        stretches to farflung corners if left unattended

    ruthlessly traps ants, lint, and miscellaneous organisms

        attracted to its liquid invert dexterity

        (indicative of striking apathetic chord)


RESPONSE TO STIMULI

    trembles under currents of avant-garde jazz suites

    displays visible bubbling annoyance when mixed

        with various rave quality substances

    unresponsive to observer's anecdotes and/or complaints

    demonstrates remarkable strength in rust removal

        (and other chelation activities)

easily bonds brick and stone
    (a shameless braggart in this and like feats of
    nonedible strength)

CONTACT WITH *h*'s (IN RASH FORM)
    clings readily to exposed skin     (rashed and unrashed)
    develops cloying attachments to midsection
    attempts dissolving exploits   over sugareaten *h*'s

PRELIMINARY CONCLUSIONS
    subject continues to maintain discrete distance from observer
    however
    would suffocate   remorseless   given the chance

## *on primping infirmity*

It is the apex of poor deportment to appear ill under any circumstances, either publicly or when receiving callers at home. This is not to say that, from time to time, our bodies do not betray us and, despite our best efforts, give in to illnesses of various kinds. However, no matter the stripe of the disease, the clever girl will find ways either to mask or to take advantage of even its most shocking effects. Regardless of the extent of medical treatment, one must take care not to flaunt any apparatus of malady. Carefully stow any paraphernalia that may confront your guests' eyes with discomfort; tuck kidney bowls, catheters, trepanation drainage pans, syringes, and other unpleasantries under the bed, or if taken by surprise or weakness, throw a handsomely stitched quilt over such devices. Manage your overt symptoms gracefully. Refrain from hacking, carping, sputtering or otherwise exhibiting uncontrolled movements or aural emanations, and for heaven's sake, take a firm grasp of any fluids, phlegms, or spittles that may be expelled from your person. Nothing will damage a reputation of refinement more than displaying (or sharing!) your pusriddled corporeity. Visible suffering repels even the most well-intentioned convalescence consorts. If you must wretch, constrict your diaphragm and ribs to temper the gesture. This will soften a virulent cough into the picture of tubercular serenity.

Ailing health is no excuse to lie about disheveled. However, primping infirmity needn't be a thorny matter. As a general rule, if a girl is lucky enough to blanch, a splash of rouge to define the cheekbone and lower lip will be sufficient. Pallors in the greenish, yellowish, or bluish hues must be firmly stamped out–liberal pancake and diamond powder should answer nicely. A thin veneer of shellac will preserve a natural tint once achieved.

Above all, remember that even a pretty convalescing peach must mind her tongue. Reroute conversations from your ailments to more palatable matters, such as the weather, the latest trends in floral arrangements, or social developments in your circle. Desist from discussing your malaise. If you cannot fully suppress your agony, internalize it to form pillars of strength, which will aid your recovery and guide your hostessing responsibilities. You may feel at the depths of ghastliness, but you needn't burden your guests with whinging. Practice and dedication allows even the most appalling invalid to present with elegance.

## Pigskin Kidney Blossoms
*mode*

Separate paired kidneys with a serrated blade
to facilitate dissection
Scoop out renal cavities and other functions
exposed by cross-sectioning
Using a swift wrist    extract ureters
Devein
Tweeze fanned nerve branches thoroughly
Dollop into fleshy gobbets
Rub each with cubed ice    and tenderness
before submerging in a cool bath
Organ morsels will blossom in chilled water

Upon scraping the underside of a sizeable
hog skinslab    tenderize with several
blunt thumps    clouts    or thwacks
Invert
Pluck stiffest bristles from the epidermal layer
by way of a sharp thumb and forefinger
Singe downier hairs
to accommodate delicate palates
seeking smoother organs
Moisturize with curled butter
Shred into wafery skinstrips
Salt-steam to soften

Combine kidney blossoms with pigskin ribbons
Sear crisp with garlic mince

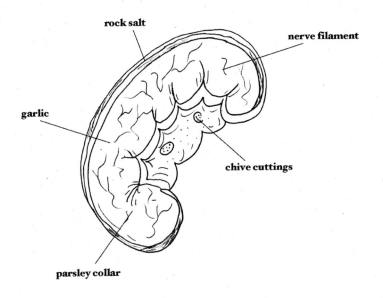

rock salt

nerve filament

garlic

chive cuttings

parsley collar

*field notes     apartment 5d*
*recorded by slug*
*evidence collected to determine the cause of the h-rash*

SUBJECT 1978: childhood memories

PHYSICAL CHARACTERISTICS
  jagged    pointed sharp
  citrus rind thick   peeled blunt    moist
  tawny edges    brittled
  yellowed tape at frayed corners

BEHAVIOUR
  twitch   twitter   fidget   in natural state
  secrete periodic gelatinous sludge
  mainly nocturnal
  peevish when ignored for too long
  flavour enhanced by mint

RESPONSE TO STIMULI
  burn in cast iron skillet      and high noon sun
  dissolve (temporarily) in tea     and most forms of alcohol
  can hold breath under cerebral fluid for up to two years
      at a stretch
      generally resurface marked by irritation
  crisp blackened naturally over time

CONTACT WITH *h*'s (IN RASH FORM)
  *h*'s murmur with discomfort
  memories appear unaffected
      primping as intriguing contagion candidates

## PRELIMINARY CONCLUSIONS

all connection to $h$'s attractive   but misleading
memories each expected to flourish in a bright flash before
   eventually
      dissipating into the atmosphere    in their own time

### "light layers": call
### featuring slug, not inflecting as he's used to

SLUG:    Look, the ground is giving way. There's no time not to be panicked. And I get it. I do.

You're upset. You feel like you have something to live for. To hold on to. Lots of people do and I don't like them any less for it. Mostly.

So it's not about that.

But you've got to pay attention to the signs. I know what you're thinking. "Oh here we go… that rash again…." Well, yeah… of course it's about that rash again. But so much more than that. It's the rumble and tickle beneath our feet. Featherlight tripwires suspended above our heads. They're falling. Getting closer. By the second.

Look, let's just go. You know? We'll live on our wits and keep moving and it will all be… amazing. Astral. Cosmological. Astrophysical. Whatever you want. We'll pack light and wear layers. Bring a sweater. A really nice one. With pearl buttons. And throw on a scarf. And something with sparkles–a brooch or a pin. And get one for me too. It'll be our emblem. There's no reason we shouldn't be decorative. And fedoras. No, forget that. That's too much.

But candy. We'll take extra candy with us. You like Flower's Kiss? We'll roll up a crate of them. That can be arranged on the fly. And we'll stuff our pockets

with sugarplums and figs and vulture kites and jacks.
Jacks will help. Especially in the early stages. The tedium
of transition.

We'll have none of that Earth Shoes and sandbags tyranny.
Forget that. It's all stilettos and sequins from here on. We'll
hole up in the crumbling clerical centres of the downtown.
The nice old brick and stone buildings, not the blocks and
towers. But that's just an aesthetic choice. It's where it's all
heading anyway... you know, after the plaster settles.

You can stutter across the exposed scaffolding. Do
somersaults off the torn awnings. You can clear your head
and finish that balancing act you've been stuck halfway
through. We can work on it together–I'll play backup on
the keypads at the ATM. We'll invite rock musicians, the
loudest ones we can find–hipster trash ones, even–to set
up their kits in the vestibules of the defunct utilities offices.
And puppeteer troupes... got to have puppets. Always.
Punch and Judy can survive anything. And mimes. No one
ever wants mimes around. But hell. Let's make them feel
welcome. Give them soup and diagonal cut toast. Let them
jitterbug with the gramophones that will be uncovered
when all the basements are exposed. And that's what it'll be
all the time... dancing on wax with bees in the pansies and
candyapples in our pockets. All that glassy red sugar and
noise and no dentists or accountants.

There's no reason it shouldn't work. None that I can think

of, right? So let's get a head start. Reach for the ground. Come on, let's *move.*

## *"arms neatly folded": answer*

BUTTERFINGERS:

it would be a grand life     probably     but for the farming issue
and what it leads to
eating fresh eggs     warm from plump ornithological bodies
and there wouldn't be any traffic     to clear the head for
considering unprecedented circumstances
which of course is always at the fore     of any decent person's front
like     the problem of a red middle     and all the disease
and injury it brings with its hulking     redness     hunkering down
the middle     a gutted fish   tingeing blue at the edges
too slightly to     vaccinate or  bloated
for polite conversation

## on minding one's head from falling beams

The world may be aflush with sulphur stuffed flaskets, but there's no reason to abandon the etiquette of civilization at the smouldering gates of our earthly incarnation.[1] In troubled times, maintain a faintly rigid posture, lest stray attitudes of permissiveness penetrate the veneer of austerity sophisticates have hitherto perfected. It may seem as though the call of the world to our Great Judge would be the time to bin our diligence in the practice of good breeding. Let's not mince about the shrubbery: it is not. It is a time to showcase your efforts all the more, not to hide them beneath a shroud of indiscretion. Though it may be the end of the world, one needn't behave as such. Think of rolling blackouts and extended power outages as an enchantingly eccentric occasion for a gathering of intimate friends. Imagine how charming a soirée the skillful hostess may lay on with an elegant set of tapers. Food prepared by aid of a kerosene cooker can be quite eloquent in the hands of a dexterous hostess.

Falling beams and crumbling sidewalks are potential hazards of limbery. Girls who remember to keep their toes pointed as they leap across widening crevasses in the pavement will survive troubled times with delicate agility, as will those who

---

1 Etiquette of this "falling beams" variety is, quite rightly, a vast area of interest, requiring much more space than our scope here may address. For further reading, see the following specialized, perforated pamphlets: *How to Accept the Help of Strangers Graciously; How to Avoid Being Duped into Corporal Payment for the Help of Strangers; How to Appear to Ignore the Sight and Sound of Crumbling Foundations, Falling Beams, and Spontaneous Bursts of Flame and Combustible Air; Where to Put One's Hands During a Blackout; How to Mind Guests' Hands During a Blackout.*

maintain a graceful shimmy rather than an oafish tumble
in the face of airborne edificial objects.

Be mindful of your escort's movements. It is not above
your dear suitor to allow a roving hand to slip beyond decent
parameters, believing the cover of darkness to be ample
excuse for this and like manual imprudence. While wild
tales of repopulation may glint with the sheen of romance,
succumbing to them will disintegrate in a blaze of shame
any strides in conduct one may have struck.

# Honeycombed Heart

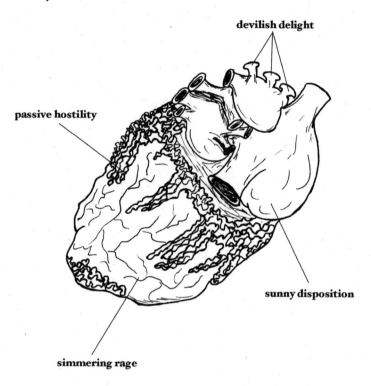

devilish delight

passive hostility

sunny disposition

simmering rage

## mode

Soak lovestruck organ in warm bath
Baste with plum bubbles and a soulful
cello melody
Peel outer membrane, layer by layer,
to expose raw musculature
Fit lips over valves, ventricles,
and other sizeable apertures
Vacuum suck
Withdraw suction popped holes from mouth,
set aside
Repeat until heart is wholly husked
Infuse honeycombed heart holes with
desired emotive blend[1]
Deepfry and roll in powdered sugar[2]

---

1 You may season with whatever emotional flavouring suits your event.
There are endless combinations, but a few suggestions for the pulmonary
novice: serenity, sweetness, and a touch of haughty pride; a hint of inse-
curity combined with anger, despair, and unrequited affection; caresses of
seduction, ruthlessness, and lust. Have fun with every dish! Experiment
with your own fusions, adjusting emotives to palate as necessary.
2 Arranged in an attractive basket, heaped honeycombed hearts make a lovely
holiday gift. Insert a candle into the centre, and you'll have the tastiest
centrepiece on the block!

### *on making the most of falling beams*

In time, gentlemen, you will learn to recognize opportunities
to engage your sweethearts more closely. Though it may
seem overbold, crass even, to make advances at the apex of
apocalyptic ruin, for instance, you are dutybound to perform
the quite necessary service of comforting loved ones. To be
a steady peg in the torrent, especially for all those twittering
tulips collapsed in petalled heaps at your doorstep. Think of
the consolation a sure hand run over a quivering thigh will
provide the fearful lily of your valley. If your shy violet has
trouble recognizing the romance of imminent destruction,
it is left to your initiative to elucidate the amorous potential
of a molten downpour and rolling hellfires. Think of all the
shudders that can be stilled with an arm wound tightly 'round
the waist. The quakes that can be assuaged with a trim peck
on the neck or a butterfly kiss on the wrist. The reptilian
rains that will fade into the backdrop with a brush of a stray
tendril from the cheek and the umbrella of a well chosen lock
on the lip. Use your ingenuity. There are endless possibilities
for soothing your blighted blossom during the last frenzied
moments pending the great void. Always be prepared, dear
sirs, to use the slightest speck of bleakery to your advantage.

### "digestible fidgets"
### featuring a scrapped-chatter chorus

SLUG:    No, but seriously, if we were to harness the sonic energy
generated from the world's bee populations, we'd have a genera-
tionally renewable clean fuel source that's thirty per cent more
powerful than wind. That's what they were saying, anyway.

BUTTERFINGERS:           buzz of consciousness    slipped
                  through the ear      lids lightpierced
      discoloured      by nocturnal exaggeration    and rem reassembly
            an archaeology of dreamworks    invites fresh lethargy
                  edged    with luscious reluctance

SLUG:    Yeah, I'm not sure how I feel about enslaving insects either.
But how exciting that it could be done.

                  smick

                        smack

BUTTERFINGERS:    chemical thinned frames    gristlestrung muscle
                        tensed fragonard over
            slender bone    pointed poseperfect
      shrivelshrunk organs slung    in stylish crêpe and satin
      lip twitters tumble  trip   cascade over hip    to angled toe    snag
                  on jagged knee

*it's all condos these days    but the decorating would be so hohumdrum*
*i just don't know what    we should do*

BUTTERFINGERS:     caviar clustered    mounded round
                       congealed frosty
    ovular enticement    tickles pinked palates black    glossy beluga
                   eggular rumble        twitch
                gumbeaded cells    crack embryonic
        larval fishes fin free from    sprigged parsley    crystalled salt
            writhe   through    rasps   undissolved  oxygen
        brush curled lip     before    toothsnap    splits    crushes
             tonguetip savours    lastgasp flavour flash
              hatch   wriggle down    peristaltic


                                        smick


                   smack


SLUG:    I see what you mean. But still, I think, eventually, we'll
    have to start relying on other food sources. Insects seem the
    natural next step.


BUTTERFINGERS:        flutter    feed  the eels    in the belly
                 cool slither    slink    gastric wrestle
        imprint the intestinal membrane shrill    gumming glutinous
        carried on plum bubbles    lubricates slickened ribbonmeat


SLUG:    Of course. Why wait until the end of the world is upon us?
    We should start to integrate it now. Freezedried cricket burgers.
    That's where it's heading.


BUTTERFINGERS:    agonizing organization of    biorhythms    and
                 scaleless crawling    digestible fidgets

smick

                smack

                                smick

*it's definitely a buyer's market     but you know the market*
*fickle as our wives*

                    smack

       smick

BUTTERFINGERS:     the promise of domestic
                   order and bliss
           drained    shelled out hollow

SLUG:    I like how retro the bomb is. Sort of romantic. But I think
   it'll be something more insidious. Microscopic....

BUTTERFINGERS:    eventually
          corners sprout fungal marvels   creatures
         emerge   potatoeyed   to run
      experiments in fertility   a dirtlush cultivation
        glittering with speed and accuracy

SLUG:   Itchy.

BUTTERFINGERS:    the taste of  time  spoiled    by vinegar solids
        caustic soda synching exotic

cotton candy feathers from accumulated food
pinking the body with brine

*if you go with the brick façade    chief    you'll save a bomb on materials*
*you can't tell the difference from the outside    looks solid as a clog*
*and pretty enough to keep the little lady    sweet*

                                    smack


                    smick

SLUG:    But once we get past all the physical torment I think it
     will be... dazzling. Raze all the infested buildings, the contagious
     infrastructure, infected architecture, to the ground and start again.

                                            smack

## "copious unsolicited post"
## featuring slow sipping litigation

SPATZ:   Another case filed crisp.

SPITZ:   Filleted and gutted, righting the scales as best we can.
What's next?

SPATZ:   A slow sipping cordial? I know a dim bistro....

SPITZ:   How 'bout another case. Nothing like diving right in,
wingtips blazing, setting the court asizzle all over again.

SPATZ:   Anything pulsing through the arteries of heartbreak
and other misdemeanors?

SPITZ:   Indeed. I've been saving this for the right moment.
You're going to love it. Have a look at this delectable case
premise.

SPATZ:   "Copious Unsolicited Post." Good title. Very
commendable. Catchy, but not too brash.

"The Plaintiff, hereafter named...." Ahem. "... hereafter
named spitz, has brought a claim against—"

You're suing me? Little old spatz from across the davenport?

SPITZ:   Genius, isn't it?

SPATZ:   They're just notes of admiration!

SPITZ:   Think of it—no dulldaisy deadweight to contend with this time. We won't even have to leave the office once we crack into the research. I'd kiss you for your missive stalking if it wouldn't skew the plaintiff's position.

SPATZ:   You understand there will have to be a countersuit.

SPITZ:   You're going to claim Lost Affection?

SPATZ:   At least.

SPITZ:   It's only natural.

SPATZ:   Have you thought what this might do to... us?

SPITZ:   We need a new project. This is a solid case. What's to lose?

SPATZ:

SPITZ:

SPATZ:   Do you have representation?

SPITZ:   Only the best. If you'll offer your services.

SPATZ:   Indubitably. And you'll represent me in the countersuit?

SPITZ:   Wouldn't have it any other way.

SPATZ:  Yes yes. I'm starting to get that prickle of intensity emanating from a career-cinching case. Have you considered all the angles?

SPITZ:  Of course. It's win-win for the firm. The absolute right fish for the hook. Just look at this file... jamthick with textual plankton. Enough evidence to send this octopus addict down the pan.

SPATZ:  As your legal counsel I'd have to concur with your complaint–this harassment cannot continue. It's just not feasible.

SPITZ:  That's what I've been trying to tell that jellyfish defendant from the outset. It's an abuse of the interoffice memo, that's certain. And verbiage beyond the pale besides. Slick pebbles of rhetoric and a jaunty phrase won't scumble the cold fact that this epistolary punk is a lexical pest.

SPATZ:  A linguistic insurgent.

SPITZ:  A syntactical charlatan.

SPATZ:

SPITZ:  An alphabetic abomination!

SPATZ:  Acting out of love, though.

SPITZ:  Certainly. But a nuisance all the same.

SPATZ:  Suppose you look at it from the other side of the postbox, for a moment... everyone should be so lucky as to have such a glistening quill-and-ink admirer.

SPITZ:  Gold! That'll really spackle my brief solid. That's the kind of shrewd legal mind we need behind us.

SPATZ:  Everything's thrillingly airtight. Let's tuck into the grit over a rapscallion geriatric stilton.

SPITZ & SPATZ:  Valises!

**Loveletters**

*spitz*

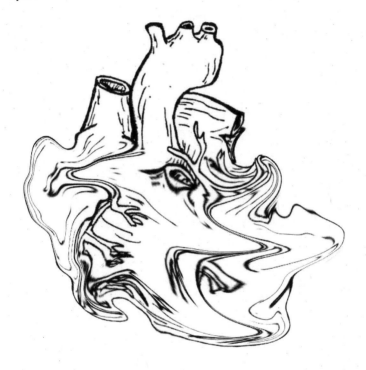

*spatz*

## Acknowledgments

Versions of some *Unisex* poems have appeared in the following publications: *Pilot: A Journal of Contemporary Poetry, P-Queue, Mad Hatters' Review, The Other Herald, LOCCAL Poetry and Public Health Placards, FOURSQUARE,* and *Phoebe: A Journal of Literature and Art.*

For essential *Unisex* contributions, heaps of gratitude to: Jason Camlot, for his whipsnap editorial precision and generosity; throwing down steady Oliver-Twistian challenges for "more"; and for wanting to take on the project in the first place. Steve Luxton and DC Books. Jeff Szuc, for the dazzling (and dead cool) cover art. Wanda Fitzpatrick, for unfaltering encouragement; reading early drafts; an *h* on the hip; and rustling up some fascinating (and appropriate) trivia about animated gophers. Jamie Popowich, for reading endless drafts of poems; sharing delicious phrases; screening a giant squid documentary at exactly the right moment; and for generally cracking wise.

For various kinds of support along the way, thanks also to: Rosa Alcalá, Mike Clody (for tripping the wings on a pretty wonderful butterfly effect early on), Davo Fiore, Mark Fitzpatrick, Rebecca Goritsas, Ming-Qian Ma, Steve McCaffery, Christina Milletti, Maggie Panko, Jeff Sirkin, Jessica Smith, Alexandra Sweeney, Ron Sweeney (for lots of things, but especially the six year (and counting) loan of that fat blue Margery Wilson book), Wendy Szczepaniak, Zenon Szczepaniak, Edwin Szczepaniak.

A doctoral candidate at the University at Buffalo, Angela Szczepaniak is neck-deep in a dissertation on innovative poetry, detective fiction, and comic books. In addition to publishing poetry and critical essays, she recently participated in a hygiene themed poetry-art project, and as a result her work can be found on placards in some of the finest public restrooms in Seattle. At the moment, she lives in Toronto.